BENN'
K. BLANC
DEE!
KOTT
CLOL
GINGRICH
JONES
HUCKABEE
MCMANUS
DUNGY
MCPHERSON
GOODE
FRANZESE
WINTER

MASTER LEADERS

CARSON
GORDON
CHAND
BARRETT
CALDWELL
TAYLOR
STEARNS
LENCIONI
GODIN
ASHCROFT
SODERQUIST
J. BLANCHARD
BLACK
MELROSE
TOWNSEND
HOLTZ

BARNA
with
DALLAS

MASTER LEADERS

Revealing conversations with 30 leadership greats

GEORGE BARNA

WITH BILL DALLAS

BARNA — AN IMPRINT OF TYNDALE HOUSE PUBLISHERS, INC.

Visit Tyndale's Web site at www.tyndale.com.

TYNDALE is a registered trademark of Tyndale House Publishers, Inc.

Barna and the Barna logo are trademarks of George Barna.

BarnaBooks is an imprint of Tyndale House Publishers, Inc.

Master Leaders: Revealing Conversations with 30 Leadership Greats

Designed by Stephen Vosloo

Published in association with the literary agency of Fedd and Company, Inc., 9759 Concord Pass, Brentwood, TN 37027.

Library of Congress Cataloging-in-Publication Data

Barna, George.
    Master leaders : revealing conversations with 30 leadership greats / George Barna with Bill Dallas.
        p. cm.
    Includes index.
    ISBN 978-1-4143-2624-5 (hc)
    1. Leadership—Religious aspects—Christianity.   I. Dallas, Bill.   II. Title.
    BV4597.53.L43B38 2009
    253—dc22   2009022877

Printed in the United States of America

15 14 13 12 11 10 09

7 6 5 4 3 2 1

CONTENTS

Acknowledgments

I owe a word (or more) of appreciation to the numerous people who contributed to converting a cool idea into a tangible reality. I am humbled by their trust in me and their desire to partner with me on this project. I offer my heartfelt thanks to:

All thirty of the master leaders who agreed to be interviewed for this book and gave me permission to use their most valuable resource—their wisdom about leadership—to help readers understand leadership better;

Bill Dallas, president of CCN and fellow long-suffering Yankee fan, for the idea behind this book and for mustering the resources to track down most of the leaders who participated in this project;

Deb Layman and Jay Mitchell, the field team at CCN who pursued many of the master leaders to solicit their participation and schedule the interviews;

Karen McGuire and Phyllis Hendry, who run the Lead Like Jesus organization with Ken Blanchard, for graciously allowing us to interview the team of leaders at the 2008 Lead Like Jesus conference, and for additional efforts to facilitate conversations with other leaders with whom they have continuing relationships;

Esther Fedorkevich, for not only serving as my trusted and very capable agent for this book, and for encouraging me when the task was looking rather bleak, but also for actively pursuing several leaders whom we eventually interviewed;

Julia Dinwiddie and Marcia Zimmerman, who joyfully and efficiently transcribed more pages of conversations than they ever imagined I'd dump on them;

Doug Knox, Jan Long Harris, Sharon Leavitt, Lisa Jackson, and Sarah Atkinson of Tyndale House Publishers for their encouragement to me and commitment to the project—and for their willingness to relax the deadline while I struggled to figure out what to do with the treasure trove of wisdom that had been accumulated for me to dispense;

David Kinnaman, Terry Gorka, Pam Jacob, and Lisa Morter, my colleagues at The Barna Group, who again covered for me while I was MIA to work on this project;

Bill and Amy Schultz, Dan and Katie Tapia, Tim and Tia Tice, Jack and Jana Woodruff, Tammy Anderson, Connie and David DeBord, Joel Tucciarone, Steve Russo, Kai Hiramine, Dona Eggar, Brant Gerckens, and Jeffrey Barsch—all of whom asked God to bless my efforts to make this a practical, helpful, and transforming book for everyone who reads it, and one that adds value to the Kingdom of God;

Nancy, Samantha, Corban, and Christine Barna, my loving family, who once again prayed with and for me about this book, encouraged me to keep going when the going got tough, took on some of my usual duties in order to free me up to meet the twice-postponed deadline, and supported me every day along the way in whatever ways they could. I love you guys more than you'll ever know, and am blessed to have a family like ours. Nancy, your encouragement after reading the first few chapters enabled me to stop holding my breath during the writing process, which significantly helped my brain functions.

Thank you, all of you. I hope you are pleased with the fruit of our joint efforts.

PREFACE

WRITING THIS BOOK WAS an unbelievable, wonderful experience. I got to spend hours and hours in the company of thirty of the nation's best leaders. Having spent more than a quarter century leading, studying leadership, writing about leadership, and teaching about leadership, I could not have asked for a more exciting and challenging opportunity.

Every quotation that you read in this book was, in fact, said by the leader to whom it is attributed.

But I have to confess something to you. The context in which their statements were made was not as this book suggests. There was no Master Leader Conference with all thirty of these leaders presenting their ideas, and there was no greenroom in which we threw out ideas and played off of each other. (There *is* a series of Master Leader Conferences that are happening across the country, featuring some of these leaders, but nobody could afford to bring all of these jewels together under the same roof—even if by some miracle we could coordinate their schedules to do so.)

No, the actual process was much more conventional. I spent time with each of the thirty stalwarts, asking them a standard series of questions and recording their answers. Overall, I prepared more than 150 questions related to more than a dozen different dimensions of leadership. I then chose a small proportion of those questions to ask a given leader, tailoring the topics to that person's areas of particular interest or expertise and the amount of time they were willing to give me. What you will read is a faithful transcription of their responses to the questions, although those replies were provided in a more intimate exchange (i.e., me and them) rather than in the interactive conversation among a group of colleagues as portrayed in the following pages.

So why did I turn to the "conversations in the greenroom" approach? Well, answer this question: Which would you find more interesting to read—a transcript of thirty one-on-one conversations addressing the same questions over and over again, or a dissection of those transcripts with the like thoughts pieced together into a virtual conversation?

After weeks of fretting about how to make all of this fabulous content come alive for readers who are generally well versed in leadership doctrine, personally engaged in the practice of leadership, and by and large, impatient and distracted, a thought flashed into my brain: create the ultimate leadership event and report what happened behind the scenes where the leaders mixed it up a bit.

Having spoken at dozens of leadership conferences over the years, I have to admit that most backstage areas at those events are dry as dust. Leaders generally enjoy being around each other, but we're usually coming off an exhausting trip to arrive at the event venue, are trying to get our heads into the topics we've been asked to address, and have half a mind focused on how and when we are getting to the next stop on the itinerary.

Occasionally, though, there is a serendipitous moment when we're all relaxed and able to enjoy each other's company. *Master Leaders* is based upon those magical moments in time, as few and far between as they may be. Hey, lightning only has to strike once, right?

As a bit of quality control assurance, after I completed the manuscript I ran it by all of the leaders I had interviewed to be sure they were comfortable with how they were represented in these conversations. After making some minor modifications, we had the content for the book you now hold in your hands.

So in a way, what we really have here is the "greatest hits" of each of these leaders. These are some of their best thoughts related to the leadership topics covered in this book. And at the risk of sounding immodest, this is the kind of book that I would want to read to get inside the heads of the people who have been mentoring me over the years and have proven beyond a doubt that they understand leadership to an abnormally robust degree.

As an author of nearly four dozen books about leadership, faith, and cultural dynamics, I have entered every book project with high hopes and pure intentions but have completed each project with various emotions. Some books felt like very positive additions to the marketplace of ideas. Others were valiant efforts but just didn't seem to accomplish what I had hoped. I am pleased to say that this is one of those books that I am very proud to have developed. It got off to a daunting start: trying to cajole a stellar list of incredibly busy, sought-after leaders to give me an hour or more of their time to capture some of their intellectual capital. Beyond that hurdle, the next hill to climb was the sheer volume of content amassed—more than five hundred pages of transcripts containing a wide range of comments. Making sense of all of that initially felt like a hopeless task. But in the end, by the grace of God, this wound up being a truly enjoyable and educational challenge that I believe will help people get their heads and hearts around the critical dimensions of leadership practice.

At one point early on in the process my publisher called and asked if the book was going to be good. When publishers have a royalty advance residing in an author's bank account, they sometimes need some reassurance that their investment was not a loony idea. Because truth is my driving value, I admitted that I didn't know if the book itself would be any good, but that I was sure learning a lot. I did not get the sense that this honesty provided the level of confidence that my publishing team was seeking. Clearly, I had not learned all of the leadership lessons imparted by my mentors, but then, I wasn't finished conducting the interviews and developing the manuscript.

Now that the book is completed, I can honestly tell them—and you—that I am excited about this resource. I believe it is readable, credible, insightful, and practical. And it is my sincere prayer that you find it to be exactly that way too.

As a recommendation, if you find a certain leader's insights particularly arresting or invaluable, I encourage you to investigate more of their thinking by reading some of their books. I have listed some of their seminal and most recent books in Appendix 2.

I hope you are neither turned off nor offended by this unusual approach to giving you easily digestible leadership coaching. What you are about to read are the hard-won insights of some of the great leaders of our age, and I hope you are able to see how each person's wisdom relates to that of other compelling leaders. I trust that you will grow from their insights and put their words of wisdom into practice.

Yours for better leadership,
George Barna
Ventura, California
June 2009

LEADERSHIP FANTASY CAMP

WHAT'S YOUR FANTASY?

I suppose we all entertain fantasies from time to time. If pressed to confess mine, I would have to include a last-second swish from the top of the key to nail down the championship for the Lakers; turning in a stellar performance on bass guitar at a sold-out concert as part of Eric Clapton's band; and penning a bestseller that becomes instrumental in transforming millions of lives.

Oh, and one more: I'd love to spend a day in conversation with the best leaders in the country to discover personal insights on how to be a better leader.

Have any of your fantasies ever come true?

Well, strangely enough, my leadership fantasy was about to come true. I had just arrived at the arena where the Master Leader Conference would be held over the next couple of days. A few months earlier, when I initially saw the lineup of leaders coming to speak at this event, I had nearly fallen off my chair. It was the cream of the crop, including renowned and proven leaders from business, politics, ministry, sports, education, the military, and the nonprofit sector. Many of them were leaders whose books I had read, whose seminars I had attended, whose journal articles and magazine interviews had captured my mind and heart over the years. They were, in a strange way, my mentors, even though I'd never met most of them. I probably knew some of their teachings better than they did.

Here's the fantasy connection. Miraculously, several months before, I had been contacted by CCN, the satellite broadcasting company that organized and would broadcast the conference to downlink sites around the nation. Bill Dallas, their president, had asked if I would be willing to serve as the master of ceremonies for the event. While he was describing the event, pitching me on the value of being associated with it, I reflected on the dozens of leadership conferences I've spoken at or attended during my lifetime. I had never been associated with anything like this. I would have been excited just to be inside the building for this spectacle! But to serve as the MC? That must have been a mistake, but I wasn't about to point out the error to the organizers.

And now in just a few hours, my fantasy would become reality.

I strode into the great cavern where the event would be held—live, in front of a few thousand people, in addition to being broadcast live via satellite to tens of thousands more. I felt a unique and dizzying blend of emotions. Blessed beyond belief. Nervous enough to vomit. Curious about what these great leaders and thinkers would reveal. Embarrassed to be on the same stage as these giants of the field. Excited about being part of such a special adventure. Horrified that the legends might discover what a poser their MC was.

I paused at the back of the auditorium to take in the sight. The simple podium, which looked like it was a mile away. The long, narrow stage, backed by fifty-foot-high crimson curtains and flanked by a pair of gargantuan video screens. The massive sound speakers dangling above the stage, chained firmly to the ceiling. Row after row of padded folding chairs on the main floor, encircled by two decks of stadium seating. Spotlights flickering different colors onto the stage as the crew tested the equipment. The muted sound of voices in the distance.

Given my duties, I realized with some disappointment that I would not be able to join the masses in any of these seats. Most of my time would be spent backstage in the greenroom, chatting up the "celebrities" before and after their appearances on the big stage. Most of them had also agreed to provide a workshop or two as well, which meant they would be spending some extra time backstage—a bonus for me! I was looking forward to having plenty of quality time with the featured speakers to kibitz about our shared interest: leadership.

This would undoubtedly be the most intense tutorial I would ever experience, an educational blitzkrieg completely unlike anything I had previously encountered. Suddenly a desperate thought crossed my mind: I should have tried to arrange for some kind of academic credit for participating in this event. But then I realized that the real world only gives credit for results, not for merely being in the presence of greatness.

And I further recognized that I needed to get a grip on reality.

Slowly, I made my way toward the stairs at the far left-hand side of the stage. I climbed the five wooden steps and stood on the platform, dead center, scanning the huge hall and absorbing the moment. In just a few hours, great things would be spoken from this very place. Things that I, and many other leaders, needed to learn from our esteemed peers.

I turned and walked into the unlit wing to the left of the stage, disappearing behind the curtains, and immediately managed to trip on a massive web of cabling that had claimed ownership of the backstage floor. As I extricated my feet, I looked up to catch the smoldering squint from one of the setup crew. He was probably twenty-five feet away, but I could feel the heat from his glare searing into me. I hurriedly cleared my way through the tangled black mess to reach the door that empties into the greenroom.

I paused in the doorway to examine the large, high-ceilinged space.

This would be my home for the better part of the next thirty-six hours. And what an inviting home it was. Spread around the room were several well-cushioned couches and easy chairs, as well as a half dozen tables hidden under crimson tablecloths, set up for dining. Five long tables covered by starched white tablecloths held silver buckets with iced drinks and trays of colorful and handsomely arranged foods. There were several large flat-screen monitors set up around the perimeter to keep us in touch with the main stage presentations. Throw in soft, recessed lighting and a faint trace of piped-in music, and you have a pretty homey environment.

As overwhelmed as I felt, I was starting to believe this was going to be fun.

Eyeing a remote corner of the room, I meandered to one of the comfortable easy chairs and plopped down, intent upon reviewing the schedule and getting my head in the game. I had intentionally arrived early—too early, really—so that I would be ready and totally focused by showtime. I pulled out the minute-by-minute schedule that the producers had provided me. But the roster of speakers was so imposing that I momentarily lost my focus. Unwisely, perhaps, I began adding up the years of leadership service logged by the group and estimated that cumulatively they had spent more than one thousand years in the leadership trenches!

Refocusing, I finished reviewing my responsibilities for the two days— introducing the speakers, thanking our sponsors, providing segues between speakers, and so forth. I had been over this time and again for the past week. There was nothing new to discover on these pages. The challenge now would simply be to execute with precision and excellence, as some of our speakers would say.

So I leaned back, took a big, cleansing breath, and rehearsed in my mind some of the questions I'd been waiting to ask these leadership Hall of Famers. Some were questions that build on the leadership research I had been conducting and writing about for a quarter century. Others were queries that some of my peers implored me to ask on their behalf.

It seemed as if every dimension of leadership practice would be addressed during the two-day event. The array of topics to be covered by our world-class experts included vision, values, and culture. Character and faith. Confrontation, conflict, criticism, and pressure. Hiring and firing, caring and motivating. Creating viable teams. Integrating moral and faith convictions into one's leadership efforts. Identifying people with leadership potential and refining the skills they need to thrive. Dealing with the dangers of wielding power. Handling criticism and pressure. Building appropriate character. Using the privilege of leadership to serve the needs of others.

Pay attention, George. Ace this test and you could rule the world!

The room was still. I knew that in a few minutes the serenity would be shattered as the stage crew, the broadcast team, and the event coordinators would rush about, and our speakers would slowly file in to get acclimated. In anticipation of that moment I closed my eyes to pray, asking for strength, clarity, and wisdom. I slowly opened them and scanned the room, hoping to record this moment in my permanent memory bank. Surely this was that brief sliver of calm before the storm hit. And with the speakers who were about to descend on this place, we were in for a Category 5 hurricane of leadership truths and principles.

I could not help but smile at the thought. Let the fun begin!

CHAPTER 1

UNEXPECTED DISCOVERIES

AS EXPECTED, ONE, THEN A FEW, then many people started coursing through the greenroom, mostly oblivious to my presence as they focused on their own pressing tasks. My nerves began to get the best of me, so I decided to do what I imagined all great leaders do when faced with pre-event jitters: eat.

I made my way to the nearest food table and began selecting pieces of sliced fruit to devour. Naturally, as soon as I stuffed the first piece of cantaloupe into my mouth, four of our guest speakers arrived. Hoping to find a familiar face, or at least to get some guidance, they stared right at me. So much for first impressions.

I quickly surrendered my plate and hurried over to greet them. Don Soderquist, who had been president of Ben Franklin, the large chain of retail stores, and, later, the longtime COO of Wal-Mart, was there. So was John Townsend, the popular psychologist and bestselling author. Tony

Dungy, the Super Bowl–winning coach was also there, alongside Ken Melrose, who had served as CEO and chairman of Toro for many years.

After welcoming them and introducing them to each other, I led the group to the food table. They chose their food and then we hit that first awkward moment—even high-powered leaders feel a little uncomfortable making conversation sometimes. It was time to break the ice.

"I am so excited to be with all of you for this conference," I began, stating the obvious. "The other speakers will all be here soon, so we'll have a lot of new faces to meet, although you probably all know each other at least by reputation. I think the audience is in for a treat these next two days."

There were murmurs of agreement, which encouraged me to plunge on. "I'm telling you, I wouldn't want to be in your shoes. You guys are positioned as the gurus of leadership." Amidst their groans of protest and mock horror, I continued. "So, tell me, over the course of your years in leadership, what have been some of the great discoveries, the 'aha' moments, that have shaped your thinking about what it means to be a leader?"

I could hear the chomping of food and the slurping of coffee as they each waited for someone else to get the ball rolling. Finally Don Soderquist smiled and launched the conversation to a great start.

"You know, one of the things I discovered is that you can't change everybody." He was immediately interrupted by a chorus of amens and then laughter. He pushed forward with his discovery. "I really believed that I could change everybody if I was honest and fair with them. I believed that if I painted a clear picture of how that individual was performing and what his or her potential was, then I could change that person.

"After a time," Don continued, "I came to realize that really I can't change *anybody*. I could counsel with them, I could coach them, I could lead them, I could hold up the mirror for them and everything. But ultimately change has to come from them. It dawned on me that if they didn't change themselves, if they didn't have the desire and the will to change, I couldn't change them."

Someone suggested that sometimes the changes that do happen are not the kinds of changes you were shooting for in the first place.

Don acknowledged the thought. "Absolutely. In fact another surprise I encountered was that people often change as they move up the organizational ladder. Egos get bigger and people become more arrogant, the higher their position. And it was a big surprise to me to see how many people at the highest level in an organization didn't know what humility means. Suddenly it was all about them. I had many examples of store managers who became district managers because they had done such a good job as store managers. But the moment they put on the coat of a district manager, they'd change for the worse. They didn't rely on what they had done well as store managers. They thought district managers needed to be tougher or needed to be different somehow. Instead of accepting the fact that they were successful because of who they were and the way they treated people, they changed all of that and struggled as a result."

I made a mental note of his point: leadership is not about your position as much as it's based on who you are as a person and the capabilities you demonstrate. Don's thoughts had clearly struck a chord with our group. There were nodding heads all around the circle of munchers. After a brief silence, Ken Melrose took up the thread.

"When I started working at Toro, the leadership model of the day was pretty much a top-down model. The big brass, the big shots with the titles, made all the decisions and told their minions what to do. As a young guy starting out, that was my model. I didn't know anything else or any executives who did things differently. But I learned that approach didn't work very well because it didn't engage the organization or create a trusting atmosphere. It emasculated employees from taking risks with new ideas."

Ken paused to take a sip of his drink, and sensing that his peers were waiting for the rest of his revelation, he ventured forth. "I eventually learned that a much better way to lead was from underneath the organization, where you're coaching and mentoring and serving the constituency and employees, trying to make them successful. If you get rid of your ego about being the powerful executive and focus on the success of others, and then they do the same with their people—so we're all focusing on the team's success instead of our own—then by virtue of the fact that they become successful, it guarantees that the boss becomes successful too. It unleashes all the potential in the employee base."

Leadership is not about one's position as much as it's based on who you are as a person and the capabilities you demonstrate.

We had now been joined by a few more speakers who had wandered in, picked up something to eat or drink, and gathered around to be part of the conversation.

Ken continued to describe his journey.

"Using that approach, our people became more trusting, they felt they could try some new things, their self-esteem went up, and they were willing to share ideas without worrying about being chewed out if they were wrong. So the whole idea of helping those people as a servant leader who focused on *them* evolved into a leadership philosophy. In essence, if the CEO behaved as if he worked for management, and management behaved as if they worked for the employees, and if employees worked to serve customers, you'd have a great organization that benefited all the stakeholders—stockholders, customers, and employees."

The sound of agreement and approval filled the room. "I bet you had a continual series of examples where the culture changed because of that leadership approach," I noted.

Ken nodded and recalled one such example, talking about one of his first experiences while he was rising through the ranks and championing that approach. "One time I had to manage a new organization within Toro that we had acquired. That company made commercial playground equipment. I didn't know anything about their business, but as I got involved it became clear that they didn't want to make any decisions because my predecessor in that company had always made all the decisions for them. Early on, the purchasing manager came to me and said he wanted to buy some steel. Their organization was kind of downtrodden and unsophisticated, and most of the employees were perfectly happy with the big boss making all the decisions.

"So the purchasing agent wanted me to tell him how much steel he should order to manufacture some swings and slides. I told him, 'Well, you're the purchasing manager; go ahead and order what you need.' He said, 'But Bob, our old boss, always made that decision for us.' I told him again that I couldn't make that decision for him. I wasn't being obstinate; I just didn't have any idea how much steel any of the equipment they made would take. But he had such low self-esteem and no confidence in his ability to make that decision.

"At that point we invited a few others from sales, inventory control, and production to join us and then went through some questions regarding what it took to make the swing, how many swings we needed to make, how much inventory we wanted to have on hand, and a few other matters. They had never done this kind of thing, getting all the people together to talk about the process and our needs.

"Pretty soon, all these people were going, 'Aha,' like it was a great revelation to them how their job was done. But it also got me thinking that even though this is just commonsense stuff, once they understood the process, you could see how it changed them. These people were sitting up straighter in their chairs. When the purchasing manager left the room, he said, 'Wow, now I know how much steel to order. We need twenty-two tons. I can do that.' I'm telling you, it looked like he was an inch taller already." He chuckled at the memory, and everyone around the table smiled at the mental portrait he had painted for us.

"That was a real aha to me," Ken continued, "because of how that simple process of empowering them lifted the employees' spirits and self-esteem. After the meeting, I sat there for a while trying to figure out what had happened that was so earth shattering. We had simply freed them to rise to the potential God had given them."

By now our circle had grown. I took a moment to welcome the newcomers and quickly introduce everyone. I hated to lose the momentum, so

I asked if anyone else had experienced such moments of insight that had altered their own views about leading.

John Townsend shared one of his discoveries. "My original concept was that a leader is someone who has the techniques and strategies to influence people in an organization to reach goals. While a leader needs those strategies and techniques, now I recognize that it's far more important that the person have two additional characteristics. One is that he or she is the right person inside, someone who has a good level of character structure and maturity—that he or she is the real deal, so to speak. And secondly, that person must know how to relate to people on an authentic and real level."

As John reached for his cup, someone asked if he had found that people with those qualities generally rise above the rest to become successful leaders.

Thinking back on his long history of interaction with leaders, John responded, "I've found that successful leaders are much more aware of their subjective, emotional responses than you would expect. My book *Leadership Beyond Reason* is all about how I learned that successful leaders are highly objective and understand data, spreadsheets, journals, research, and all the diligence they are supposed to have to influence people and make decisions. *But,*" he said with emphasis, "the really successful leaders also pay attention to their guts, intuition, hunches, emotional reactions, passions, and creativity—all of that soft-science, subjective stuff. They really give a lot of attention to that input, and it gives them the wealth of information they need in a complex organization. Now, because I believe that God made reality to be integrated, so that truth is truth whether it is objective or subjective, I believe those leaders are able to make far more discerning judgments about decisions because they can listen to their guts as well as their heads."

While a few speakers echoed John's sentiments, I welcomed Barry Black, who serves as chaplain of the U.S. Senate; Ken Blanchard, the world-renowned management and leadership expert; Miles McPherson, pastor of a megachurch in San Diego; and Sam Chand, a former college president currently engaged in leadership consulting around the world. By now we had about one-third of our total group of speakers in the room.

For those just joining us, I explained that I had been asking people about some of their aha leadership moments. I summarized how some of our colleagues had discovered that leadership is less about commanding and more about empowering people to live up to their potential by using all of their abilities.

Sam Chand chimed in almost immediately. "I'll tell you," he said with a characteristic mischievous gleam in his eye, "on my journey I have discovered some defining things, and one of them is how little I can do by myself and how much more I can do through others. I discovered that I was perpetuating a vicious cycle of not developing other leaders. I was born and raised in a pastor's home in India, and eventually became a pastor, then a college president, but I have yet to have somebody put his arm around me and say, 'Sam, I see some gifts in your life, some talents. Let me take you under my wing and mentor you. There's no use in you making the same mistakes I made.' That has not happened in my life, and so I began perpetuating the same cycle. When I left the church I was leading in Michigan, it was then that I realized I had not really grown people because I did not know how to grow people. Once I realized I needed to be intentional about how to do that, I became a student of it, and that's much of what I do now."

Leadership is less about commanding and more about empowering people to live up to their potential by using all of their abilities.

I related well to Sam's tale. Growing yourself as a leader is one thing; knowing how to help other people reach their leadership potential is something else altogether. It really does take a willingness to focus on others rather than self. Meanwhile, Chaplain Black offered one of his "lightbulb" moments.

"As my understanding of leadership has evolved, I have come to see leadership as far more collaborative than I had previously suspected. Earlier I had a more heroic model of a leader. I saw great leaders like John Kennedy and Martin King and assumed that the power of their charisma enabled them to get people to do whatever they articulated in their speeches or in their writings. As the years have gone by, I have come to think of leadership as the mobilization of people toward a shared objective. And that mobilization requires the leader to first listen in order to learn, in order to lead. It does not mean that you do not have an individual vision. Nehemiah knew he wanted to rebuild the walls, but he still listened in order to learn before he started to lead the people. So leadership has become far more collaborative in the later stages of my experience than in the early stages."

This line of reasoning got Ken Blanchard's juices flowing. He was enthusiastically nodding as Barry spoke. Ken seemed eager to build on the foundation the chaplain had laid. It didn't surprise me; Ken has been a leading champion of collaborative leadership models for years.

"When I first started, and even when *The One Minute Manager* came out, there was much more of a hierarchical view of organizations, where the manager took the lead in setting the goals and deciding whom to praise and whom to reprimand and redirect. Today I look at leadership much more as a partnership than any kind of hierarchical arrangement. Young people in particular are fascinated when you talk to them about the shift in thinking. They just can't believe that we ever used the term 'superior.' And who works for superiors? Well, subordinates—you know, sub-ordinary people. And then they get a big kick out of saying: 'What's your role?' I'm in supervision. 'Well does that mean you see things a lot clearer than these stupid people that work for you?' So I think it's much more of a partnership now, and we spend a lot of time talking about partnering for higher performance. A big aha for me was to realize that all the effective aspects of leadership are about servant leadership—about serving your customers and serving your people."

Ken had written a series of popular books on that very transition in his thinking and in the field of leadership. He would be speaking on the topic of servant leadership later in the conference. That was clearly his sweet spot—well, one of them.

I noticed that Tony Dungy and Miles McPherson were joking with each other off to the side. It wasn't surprising that they resonated with each other: Miles had played professional football prior to immersing himself in full-time ministry, and Tony has always been very active in pursuing his Christian faith. After Ken had finished, I asked them what they were rattling on about.

"Just sharing stories," Miles gushed. "I'll tell you, though, one of my 'aha' moments was when I recognized that I could get more out of people by encouraging them. I'm a motivator in the pulpit. I encourage people; I'm positive and funny and all that, but when I would come away from the pulpit, I didn't manage people that way. I'd manage them more forcefully, reminding people that we had a lot of work to do so let's go, go, go. The aha for me was that if I encourage people to do a great job, they will try harder and then, if I tell them they've done a great job, it produces even more good. Encouragement produces a better worker and a happier worker and a more motivated person. So I had to work on translating the kind of encouragement I normally give from the pulpit into a more consistent leadership practice, which is something I wasn't doing."

Tony, who is a man of quiet intensity, nodded his head and then spoke up.

"I have had the benefit of working under several very good leaders with different styles. I got to observe different types of leadership. When I first came into coaching football, I thought the leader of the team—the coach as the leader—was a guy who had to be very commanding and demanding. For the most part that was the role model that I had seen while growing up. And then I saw leadership carried out more as teaching and nurturing. So I began feeling that the leader of our football team was the person who needed to keep everybody going in the right direction and in the same direction, someone to keep the focus and priorities. But it was not necessarily about pushing people to go the way you want them to go. The big change for me was getting to a point of understanding that leadership is really about getting people to follow you as opposed to you having to push them in a direction you want them to go."

A bunch of speakers piped in after those comments, agreeing that effective leadership is about motivating people to be part of a collaboration in which everyone has a stake and the leader is simply directing the flow of energy and talents toward a specified, agreed-upon goal.

As I looked around, I realized with great satisfaction that it was as if we were building a great team right there in the greenroom! All these tremendous leaders appreciated the insight that each of the others brought to the forum, and we seemed to have a shared sense of what leadership was about. And everyone, so far, had admitted that his understanding of great leadership had either been born from mistakes he had made or misimpressions he had been taught and had to overcome.

Just then, the door burst open and the rest of our speakers marched in. I went over to shake hands, make introductions, and do the host thing. By this time the positive vibe that had been established in the room had melted away my previous anxiety. Here I was, among many of my personal leadership heroes, having a great time getting to know them, hearing their stories, and learning from their years of experience and study. That was one of the lessons I would take away from the day. Not only do leaders enjoy being in the company of other leaders, and talking about the subject they have come to love, but they usually have a storehouse of tales gleaned from years in the field.

Note to self: leaders teach through stories, even if the tale is told at their own expense.

The floor director found me in the midst of a group of leaders and pulled me aside, imploring me to put on my mic and get ready to go onstage to get things rolling.

It was showtime!

CHAPTER 2

DEFINING AND EVALUATING REAL LEADERSHIP

I RETURNED TO THE greenroom stoked! The house was packed, the audience was full of energy and enthusiasm, and we had the world's best lineup of leaders to supply them with everything they needed to take their game to the next level.

So with the proceedings now underway I figured that my role was to keep the speakers comfortable while making sure they had a working knowledge of what was happening onstage. That would be a bit of a balancing act, but hey, if this is suffering, put me down for the maximum dose.

I unobtrusively visited each flat-screen monitor in the greenroom to be sure they were operating properly. While doing so, I heard our opening speaker, former attorney general, governor, and U.S. senator John Ashcroft, lay down some basics for the rest of the conference. As he set up the crowd to receive his definition of leadership, I automatically recited my own description in my mind:

Leadership is motivating, mobilizing, resourcing, and directing people to pursue a shared vision that produces positive transformation.

It is a definition I have used in books, presentations, and training exercises. More importantly, it has been the touchstone for my own adventures in leadership, as I have tried to partner with people in creating a better future. Anxiously I awaited John's description. It didn't take long.

"First, leadership is the identification of noble goals and objectives," he began, "and, second, it is the pursuit of those noble goals and objectives with such intensity that others are drawn into the process. The difference between a con man and a leader is that the con man can talk people into pursuing the goals at greater levels of commitment than he has himself.

Leadership is motivating, mobilizing, resourcing, and directing people to pursue a shared vision that produces positive transformation.

"When I was in high school and college, I was an athlete. There were guys in the locker room who would bang on the lockers and yell, 'We're going to go out there and kill them.' And then, as soon as we got outside the locker room, they would offer to hold my coat. You see, a leader is the person who pursues noble goals with such intensity that others are drawn to those goals. Leadership is taking people where they are not already going. It is about redefining the possible."

I wanted to pause to reflect on John's definition, but he continued his presentation.

"I have come to understand that leadership is different from governance. Some people confuse the two. Governance is the process whereby minimums are established. In government, the law is passed, and it sets the minimum threshold for activity. If you don't exceed that threshold, you are the subject of impositions and mandates. Leadership is different from governance because it doesn't establish the lowest and least that is acceptable, but it inspires people to their highest and best. Whereas governance operates on the basis of mandates, imposition, punishment, and things like that, leadership operates on the basis of models. The outcome of governance is the establishment of a floor. The outcome of leadership is people operating at their highest and best."

It seemed as if John was using the term *governance* in a way that is parallel to the way many use the term *management*. I felt his distinction was a helpful push toward our understanding of leadership.

I noticed that a couple of other speakers were taking in John's presentation too. I asked Laurie Beth Jones, the bestselling author and leadership coach, how she would have defined leadership if she were onstage right now.

"I think of leadership as the ability to persuade others to accomplish things together. It is getting people to go along and work together to accomplish something, being able to persuade others around what needs to be done and making that happen."

"That's pretty much on par with John's view," I noted. "Have you always had that same perspective, or has it evolved as you've had more diverse experiences in leading and coaching?"

"Well, I used to think that leadership was all about motivation. I thought that to be a good leader you had to be a great speaker and be eloquent. There are certain personality types that will respond to that. But there are other personality types, certain groups that are not going to be motivated just by beautiful words and high-energy speeches. They are going to take a more measured approach. So I discovered that leadership is really the ability to get people with different personalities and different value sets to agree on what is important and move forward. It's a science, as well as the art of beautiful speech-making."

Jon Gordon, one of the new voices on the leadership scene and a popular consultant to a wide-ranging clientele, piped in.

"What great leaders do really well is communicate a clear, consistent, and simple vision that everyone in the organization can rally around. A great example is Doug Conant, the CEO of Campbell Soup Company." I quickly rifled through my memory to place that name. I recalled that he had been the president of Nabisco before accepting the CEO position at Campbell's nearly a decade ago. He was well regarded in leadership circles as an astute and capable leader.

Jon continued his thought. "Doug said the most important thing he does as a leader is to share the mission and vision of Campbell Soup Company wherever he goes. I think one of the main things a leader does is to share the vision and the mission of the organization: why they are in business, why they do what they do, why the organization is here, and what they are driving toward. And that means leaders need to move their organization to define their bigger purpose. These days, people are looking for meaning. They want their work to have a greater purpose. And we know people are more energized when they are using their strengths for a bigger purpose beyond themselves. You have to show people what, why, and how the work they are doing is moving them toward fulfilling a bigger purpose. A good leader will help define that for people."

As our discussion expanded to encompass more people, someone stated that it can be dangerous for a leader to try to impose his or her vision on the group. Jon smiled in agreement and responded.

"Leadership is not about what you do as the leader, but about what you can inspire or encourage or empower others to accomplish. Leaders bring out the best in other people by sharing the best from within themselves. Just because you are driving the bus doesn't mean you have the right to run people over. Abraham Lincoln said almost anybody can withstand adversity; but to test a man's character, give him power. Leadership is knowing that you have power but your responsibility is to serve, develop, and empower others."

Sam Chand was enthusiastic about the course of the conversation.

"I'm right there with you, Jon," he said approvingly. "To me, leadership is seeing the needs in other people's lives and being willing to move into their lives with intentionality. My personal vision is to help others succeed, because I think real leadership is never about you getting the job done; it is helping others do what they can do best."

I saw a chance to stir a bit of controversy and asked Sam if that meant that a leader's ultimate success was outside his or her own control.

"Look, when we are talking about leadership, success is not the same kind of 'success' that I read about in popular literature. Leadership is about saying, 'God, You placed me on the planet, there's a purpose for each of us, so please put me in touch with the right people in whom I can invest my life so that when they succeed, I can succeed along with them.' You see, George, my success depends on their success."

Seth Godin, the iconoclastic voice on matters relating to leadership and marketing, was standing along the outside edge of the group, following the exchange. Knowing that Seth is a brilliant thinker and had recently written a book (*Tribes*) that put a different spin on leadership, I invited him into the dialogue.

"But Seth," I said, teasing him, "didn't you write that all a leader does is gather people together and orchestrate what they really want?" It was neither a complete nor fair description of his thesis—and I knew it—but I wanted people to hear his ideas and hoped that such a challenge would highlight his distinctive perspective.

"First of all," he began, "leadership is mostly about connecting people both to each other and to a future that they want to see. It is rarely about the characteristics or personality or traits of the leader. *People* magazine would have us believe that celebrities and leaders are the same thing, but they're not.

Leadership is mostly about connecting people both to each other and to a future that they want to see.

"What leaders do is indulge the ego in the follower—ego in the best possible sense—and help followers realize something in life that they've wanted to do for a long time. What leaders do is to amplify the desires of the people of their tribe by reflecting them back to each other.

"Barack Obama is a perfect example of this. Many people have criticized him for being sort of an empty vessel, and you can see in him what you want. But in fact, one of the traits of great leaders is that they allow you to see yourself. And then when you hear yourself played back through them, it makes yourself louder. And when you hear other people around you saying what you're saying, it makes it louder again. And that gives you the courage to do the next thing.

"So leading is about delaying personal gratification," Seth concluded. "The sales culture of our country and our world says you need to get paid first. In fact, leaders get paid last. If you wait for your turn, the payoff is far greater than if you take your return first."

I loved that notion of leaders not simply helping people to identify, pursue, and realize their dreams, but also not being successful until those outcomes have been reached. In an instant-gratification society, where so many people are held up as paragons of leadership simply because they had a great idea or made some bold statements, the idea of facilitating greatness before being publicly regarded as great resonated deep within me.

Sam and Seth had touched on a critical element of understanding genuine leadership. "So what, then, is success in leadership?"

Sam immediately responded, "I look at the people I'm working with and look for growth in their lives in becoming more other-ward, more other-focused. Success is for a leader to see the need and the potential in others, come alongside them, and help them do what they need to do and go where they need to go."

I couldn't help but smile as Lou Holtz, the legendary football coach, cleared his throat and adjusted his glasses. If anyone understood success in leadership, Lou was certainly on that team. Here was a man who had taken over a hapless Notre Dame football team and turned it into a national powerhouse almost overnight—without having the most talented players on the planet. He'd had similar incredible outcomes in other places, as well. And I always appreciated Lou's self-effacing, humble way of looking at himself and his accomplishments.

"I think success as a leader is getting people to achieve things that they didn't think were possible on their own. We all have more talent and ability than we think, but we need somebody who really believes in us, and sets goals and standards, and shows us how we could possibly achieve them. I think there are too many people in a leadership role that are worried about being popular. Woody Hayes was a great leader. The guy was difficult to work with sometimes, he was cantankerous, and he was short." People laughed as they hung on Lou's words. "But anybody who played for him would die for him, and anybody who coached for him would die for him, including me. Why? Because he cared about his people and he wanted you to be the best you could be. He didn't care whether you liked him or not. I'll never forget him saying, 'Your role as a coach is not to be well liked by the players. Your role is to make them the very best that they can possibly be.' Plain and simple. You can't worry, in a leadership role, whether you're popular or well liked, and you can't worry about what the media says. Your job is to help people reach their potential."

"I really like that," added Erwin McManus, the creative force behind Mosaic, a community of faith in Los Angeles, and a sharp thinker on matters of leadership and cultural change. "But the word *successful* always throws me off, you know? I have a sense that you can't measure your life against anyone else; that's the kiss of death. You just need to be able to go to bed at night and know that based on who you are and who God has made you to be, you've contributed the greatest good that you can for the good of others. And that when you get up in the morning you can't wait to get out of bed because there's this eager anticipation that your life can be a gift to the world. Life is a gift. When you receive it as a gift you begin to give yourself as a gift."

Erwin has had an unconventional career, and he introduced some of that background by way of explanation. "I pastored a church among the urban poor for six years. My average income was six to eight thousand dollars a year. That was the total package: salary, benefits, and everything combined. And I never saw more than two hundred people walk into that community of faith. I thought I was successful until everybody told me I wasn't. I woke up in the morning and would see someone who was a drug addict or someone who had been a prostitute or someone whose whole family was in disarray because of drug abuse. And when I saw things come together in their lives, and there was wholeness and healing, I thought I was successful. It was actually Christians who later explained to me that that was not success." Our little crowd laughed at—and resonated with—his recollection. "So I think the best way of measuring success is just assessing the good you're doing in the lives of others."

Recognizing that we had people from such disparate walks of life on the team—business, ministry, education, military, and so forth—I asked if perhaps there were different ways of gauging success based upon what kind of activity a person was leading.

Never one to shy away from a tough question or difficult situation, Miles McPherson voiced his thoughts.

"You know, for me, and this might seem too simple, but I measure success by my level of obedience to God. The way I look at it, my job is to plant seeds and to water those seeds, and if I do what I'm supposed to do, how I'm supposed to do it, then God produces the growth. Before, I tried too hard to produce the fruit and then measure the results. But now, success is figuring out if I used my time and energy today the way God wanted me to use it or if I wasted it. If I used my time in the way God wanted me to, I can go to bed happy and lie down at peace with God. Getting that straight was important for me, because if success is about making people do what I want, then I will do one thing, but if it's about being obedient, then I'll probably be doing something else."

Barry Black spoke to that issue.

"I think success involves at least three things for a leader, no matter what you're leading. The first thing is faithfulness. 1 Corinthians 4:2 says it is required of servants that they be found faithful. And in the parable of the talents in Matthew 25, the commendation is not 'Well done, good and successful servant' or 'Well done, good and talented servant' but 'Well done, good and faithful servant.' I believe that God measures our effectiveness by our faithfulness. Are you reliable? Are you dependable? That's what I think faithfulness means. Second, I believe that you are successful when your leadership glorifies God. In fact, Jonathan Edwards, the great Christian writer, said his first resolution was that whatever he did would glorify God. And 1 Corinthians 10:31 says, "Whether you eat or drink, or whatever you do, do all to the glory of God." So the issue is whether or not my leadership is glorifying God. And finally, a corollary of that is that you're successful when you please God. When I am leading in such a way that I know God is pleased with my work, then I'm successful, regardless of what the world might think."

But what if the results produced don't reach the level expected, or they don't compare favorably with what other leaders produce?

"Remember," the chaplain grinned, "Noah preached for 120 years and was only able to convince seven people to go into the ark with him. And yet he was successful, I believe, because he was faithful. His leadership glorified God, and his leadership certainly pleased God."

As the conversation took a breather, we could hear the words from the platform over the speakers. Former governor and presidential candidate Mike Huckabee had joined John Ashcroft onstage, and the pair bantered about leadership in the trenches. To my surprise, Huck began talking about the issue of success in leadership. Coincidence? I think not.

"Success is essentially having clearly defined goals and meeting them with integrity," Huck was telling the spellbound audience. "And integrity is an important part of it, because if you gain the world and lose your soul, that's not success. I have seen it in politics. They got what they wanted, but what it took to get there was not what they wanted to be, and then it was too late. You know, there are a lot of things you can get back, but your reputation, well, that's not one of them. It's a dangerous thing to want something so badly that you start selling out to get it, compromising your core values."

Huck identified one of the critical elements of successful leadership: staying true to your core values. That was an idea that Don Soderquist wanted to emphasize.

"Leaders really are the standard setters as far as values in an organization.

The values are the foundation of behavior within an organization and within the development of organizational culture, and it is critical that the senior leaders are the champions of values. And it is just as critical that they are the ones who effectively model what those values are."

Watching the monitor carefully so I wouldn't miss my time cue for returning to the stage to transition from John and Mike to our next speakers, I heard Henry Cloud offer some closing thoughts on success in leadership. Henry's blockbuster books about leadership and life success are based on his extensive counseling experience as well as years of executive coaching in business and ministry environments. I sensed he was carefully trying to bridge any gap between those who led in a for-profit setting and those whose work was performed in a nonprofit atmosphere. And that was just what we needed at that moment: a view that would take us beyond the idiosyncrasies of specific settings and tie together all the valuable insights we'd already heard into a practical, universal perspective.

"Every leader, in a sense, has got to establish some metrics of how he or she defines success in whatever his or her particular mission is. So in some ways the content of those measures will differ. But transcending that, I think if you look at all of the leadership literature, if you look at all of the leadership experience out there, you'll always find the same two things. There is relationship and there is task."

"What does that mean?" someone asked.

"Well, in other words, when leaders are successful, in the wake of their leadership you're going to find people who were better off for having been under or with or alongside their leadership. They've grown, they've developed, they've been touched, they've been inspired, they've been challenged, they've been corrected, they've been built. That leader has left people behind who are better off for having been there. That's one side."

Henry scanned the group, and seeing that they were tracking with his train of thought, finished his explanation. "The other side is that whatever the mission was, it was accomplished. You know, we can be good with people—that's the relationship part—but did we really end up fruitful at the end of the day? That's the task part.

"I think that every organization and every leader ends up defining success differently because of the peculiarity of their own mission. But there's got to be fruitfulness in what they were there to do, and it's got to be done in a way where people have been bettered in the process. If you look at it from a biblical point of view, related to the people side of it, you might identify success by whether people have been made more complete in the image of God and whether people are living the essence of the gospel. And then on the task side, you'd look to see if in some way, either overtly or otherwise, the Kingdom of God has been moved forward because of that leadership."

By this time I had completely lost sight of my role as a host while I contemplated Henry's words about success. Fortunately, one of the stage managers rushed over to alert me to the need for me to get to the wing of the platform, since Huck and John were wrapping up their session.

As I made my way out of the greenroom toward the stage, I realized that while my fantasy of hearing the best thoughts of America's great leaders was being realized, I was going to need a lot of time to process those insights. Some of what I was hearing was confirming my preexisting views, some was adding breadth to those views, and some was outright clashing with my beliefs about leading. Regardless, these were all people whose experience, intelligence, and commitment to the advancement of leadership demanded that their views receive my serious consideration, no matter how uncomfortable that might feel.

After all, the goal of the Master Leader Conference was not to coerce everyone to embrace the same thoughts. The desired result was for each of us to be sufficiently challenged by each other so that we would become the ultimate leaders we are meant to become. Great leadership, like life itself, is a journey of process, experience, and growth, more than a final destination that is likely to be reached.

CHAPTER 3

VISION AND VALUES

THE CONFERENCE WAS RUNNING on all cylinders. John Ashcroft and Mike Huckabee had done a great job during the opening session of getting people focused by providing some humorous but insightful insider stories about their leadership challenges in government. After introducing our next session and speakers, I hightailed it back to the greenroom. The conversations happening there had gotten my juices flowing and triggered a new set of questions to pose. I couldn't wait to get back to the ultimate cocktail party (without the cocktails, of course) and keep the wisdom flowing. By this time the room had divided into several small circles of leaders clustered around the food tables. I reached the nearest one, greeted everyone again, and listened to some small talk. After a couple of minutes, I plunged forward with a question.

"You know, for a while all anyone talked about was the importance of vision. But so far today I have not heard anyone in here talking about vision. Is that a passé concept? Have we worn out the topic, or said everything that needs to be said about it? It seems to me that vision is still the starting point for any kind of successful leadership venture. What do you folks think?"

"The key thing that a successful leader is able to do is to create a vision that people can get behind," responded Ben Carson, the brilliant neurosurgeon who had recently been named by *Business Week* as one of the most influential people in the world. "The book of Proverbs says, 'Where there is no vision, the people perish' (29:18, KJV). This is a time when we need leadership that can help the people understand who we are and not try to sanitize everything and make it acceptable to everybody so that absolutely nobody could possibly be offended about anything. That's not what beliefs and values are about. Beliefs and values are about knowing who you are and being able to tolerate and accept other people, but without changing who you are at every whim."

The people in our group seemed pretty comfortable with that diagnosis—except for Seth Godin. Leave it to Seth to challenge the conventional thinking—even if Ben's "conventional" thinking was not really a conventional practice. I knew from our research among leaders across the country that vision gets a lot more lip service than real service. Most leaders do not have a vision that drives their organization; they're more likely to be focused on reaching financial targets or maintaining a high corporate profile than they are to propose and pursue a unique and compelling reason for being. And our studies had discovered that in many of the organizations that have a vision statement, those words have merely become slogans that appear on letterhead and signage but have little real effect on the decision making or heartbeat of the organization.

So Ben's good thoughts were probably more insightful than they might at first appear. But Seth was going to have a good-natured go at it anyway.

"You know, if you watch enough Hollywood movies, it certainly seems like leaders have a full vision from the beginning and then it unfolds exactly the way they thought it would," Seth explained. "But in fact, that's not true at all. Yes, Berry Gordy had something of a vision as he started leading Motown and breaking the color barriers in the music business. But I don't think he ever could have described for you what Motown was going to look like.

"True leadership is not necessarily about having a concrete vision of what the end will be like. It's embracing the process of what a group is going to go through to get to wherever the group is going. And too often people hesitate to lead because they don't know what the end will bring. But, in reality, leaders *never* know what the end is going to bring. They just know that there's a process they're willing to embrace."

As his contrarian thinking often does, Seth's assessment got the group engaged. The next one to speak was Ken Blanchard, whose gentle, grandfatherly way always diffuses the heat and gets to the meat.

"You know, most organizations don't have a vision statement, or a mission statement, or a set of operating values, or any of that," he stated. It was exactly what I'd found in our research, but how much better is it to have one of the revered grand statesmen of leadership studies make the case for you? "Organizations ignore those things and then they wonder why they lose their direction. But you see, if you don't get that piece right as a leader, then your leadership doesn't matter, because leadership is supposed to be helping people go somewhere specific.

"I learned from Jesse Stoner, who has been studying the power of vision for several decades, that there are really three parts to a compelling vision. One is determining who you are, or knowing what business you're in. The second is knowing where you're going, which is your picture of the future. And the third is figuring out what will guide your behavior, which is specifying your values. So a compelling vision tells you who you are, where you're going, and what will guide your journey. And once you're clear on those things, then you could put goals under those, but at that point the goals have some meaning because of the context supplied by the vision."

I thought I saw where he was going with this. "In other words, the vision has to represent how you convert your passion into productive action that's consistent with your core beliefs?"

Ken nodded in afirmation and said, "Let me give you an example. I was working with a big bank a while back and they sent me their mission statement. I got up in front of the president and everybody and said, 'I really appreciate getting your mission statement because I've gotten much better sleep since I got it. I put it next to my bed, and if I can't sleep I read your mission statement, because it's so wordy and it couldn't motivate a flea. Look, I'm a customer of banks. I would hope that you'd be in the peace-of-mind business. If I give you my money I'll want to have the peace of mind that comes from knowing you'll take my money, protect my money, maybe even grow my money.'

"Why didn't Walt Disney say that he was in the theme park business?" Ken had a rapt audience at this point. "He said, 'We're in the happiness business.' You see, you need a rallying call. Jesus said, 'I'm going to make you fishers of men.' He didn't say, 'Let me give you my mission statement.' And I've found that if Jesus does it, then it's probably the thing you ought to do."

As our group chuckled along with Ken, he made his argument even more practical. "So the first thing to do is find out what you're really doing. We worked with the big baseball stadium in San Diego. The owners wanted the fans to have a good time and a wonderful experience. Their mission now is simple: the only reason they exist is to make good memories. What's so neat about that is everybody, whether as part of the food service or ticket sales, knows that what they are trying to do is make a positive memory for the customer. So when it comes to vision, that's the first thing you've got to do."

Ken was doing something else that I've noticed great leaders do: take the complex and make it simple. He went on to further explain the visioning process.

"Then the picture of the future is figuring out if you accomplish your vision, what will happen? With Disney, the picture of the future is that all the guests leaving the park will have the same smiles on their faces they had when they entered the park six, eight, ten, or twelve hours ago. You take your vision and make it a rallying call by asking, 'If we do a good job, what will happen?' At the stadium in San Diego, Petco Park, the picture of the future is that every fan leaving the game will be talking with those they came there with about who they're going to bring next time. I took my grandsons to a Padres game early on when we started working with them. We were coming out after the game, and my oldest grandson, who was ten years old, said, 'Grandpy, when are we coming again?' I asked him why he wanted to know, and he said, 'Because I'd love to bring Grant. I think he would really enjoy this.' That's his best buddy.

"And the third component is your values. If you've identified your picture of the future, then what are the values that are going to drive that behavior? Most organizations, if they do have values, have too many—eight, ten, twelve. You know, they're for God, mother, and country, and so forth. The Pharisees said to Jesus, 'Ten Commandments? Too many. What are the biggies?' And so He said, 'These two,' and He even rank ordered them! So again, I think if Jesus did it, it's worth doing.

Great leaders take the complex and make it simple.

"I think the reason your values have to be rank ordered is that life is about value conflicts. Going back to the Petco Park example, when we worked with the Padres, we got all the employees, twenty-five hundred of them, down on the field Sunday after the first home game. They never thought they'd be on the field. And then we had them walk the four bases, and at each base was a sign that had a rank ordered value. The sign at first base said, 'Safety.' Why? Because if somebody gets carried out of here on a stretcher, he's not going to have a great memory. So safety has got to be number one.

"Second base was 'Service'—you know, being courteous and friendly. It's good to know it's second, but why is it important to rank order the values? Well if I'm answering somebody's question in a friendly, courteous way and I hear a scream and it's not coming from the field, I've got to dismiss myself immediately and follow the scream. But suppose it's a good-looking woman, you know. And I'm thinking, *I wonder what she's doing after the game,* and I hear a scream and I say to myself, *Oh, it's no big deal, they're always screaming in the park.* And they come to me later on and say, 'You were closest to the scream. Why didn't you move?' 'Well, I was dealing with service.' But you see, you don't deal with service if this is a safety issue.

"Third base was 'Fun.' One of the employees said, 'Remember when you were young and you went out on a date, if you had a good time on the date, what's the chance your date had a good time? Pretty good. But if you had a lousy time, what's the chance your date had a good time? So if we're having fun doing our jobs, what's the chance the fans are going to have fun? But if we're not having fun and we're saying, "When's the stupid game going to be over?" well, that's a problem.'

"And then home plate was 'Success': having a profitable, well-run organization. Most organizations don't have anything about their financial well-being as a value. And if you don't have it there, then your values are a joke, because the minute the finances are tight, everybody's spending a lot of time focused on them. But the fact that it's fourth says that at Petco Park they're not going to do things to save money if it puts people in danger. Why not? Because safety is number one. They're not going to have a major downsizing in the park because you can't have courteous, friendly service if nobody can find a person who can help them.

"If organizations get those three components—knowing what their business is, picturing the end result, and ranking values—and communicate them, everybody can understand them. Then, when you put it up on the wall, it has some meaning. And then you put the goals under that and they just come alive. It's really powerful."

Ken had just given us a primer on developing vision. And true to form, I saw the leaders around me light up in reaction to a discussion about vision. In some ways, it's a topic that has been talked to death. In other ways, though, vision is the air that leaders breathe, and they cannot help but get excited when they relate the idea of vision to their own calling to lead.

Newt Gingrich had been listening closely to Ken's words and affirmed them almost immediately.

"What a wonderful example," commented the grinning former Speaker of the House. "You did the very thing that we've found to be critical in the political world: you began by defining your values—those in you and those of the people you're trying to lead. Then you hammered out a vision of how to achieve those values. You asked how you were going to get it done: *This is what I believe in, now how will I do it?*"

Then Newt added a new idea. "In the process, metrics are important because you have to figure out in the real world whether or not your vision and values are happening. I studied Peter Drucker and Edward Deming and realized that for that to happen you have to learn whatever you need to learn. I'm endlessly trying to figure out what it is I don't understand. When you get the metrics figured out, if you know you need to achieve these metrics in order to achieve this vision and these values, then what are the strategies that will achieve these metrics? Then you ask what projects you need to facilitate."

Vision is the air that leaders breathe.

So now we were reflecting on the blending together of several endeavors: clear and practical vision, a handful of indispensable values, some objective measurements to discern where things stand and where they need to go, and the development of a plan to get there. As a researcher, I was especially pleased to hear Newt promote the significance of metrics. Over the years I had become acutely aware of how few leaders were serious about defining and objectively measuring performance in light of the vision and values. His comment reminded me of one of the core principles I always try to leave with our clients: you get what you measure.

One of the people in our group was Rich Stearns, the visionary leader who had demonstrated his capacity to make vision real in a variety of settings. As president of Parker Brothers, then Lenox, and currently leading World Vision, the global Christian relief and development organization, Rich has witnessed the power of vision firsthand for more than three decades. He jumped on the bandwagon to help tie together the communication and evaluation aspects that Ken and Newt had just alluded to.

"I've found, especially in my ten years at World Vision, that vision casting is even more important when you're involved in a great cause and you're mobilizing not only your employees, but your donors and the public, to embrace that cause. You've got to find words that motivate and ways to paint pictures that bring people together on the same page. Years ago we did a research study about attitudes of evangelicals toward HIV and AIDS." Rich turned to his left and spoke directly to me. "George, I think your comment to me at the time was, 'I wouldn't want your job. The American public seems to have not only no interest and compassion around this issue, but they also have a negative feeling about HIV and AIDS.'"

You get what you measure.

I recalled conducting that research study for World Vision. It was the first study I had conducted for them since Rich had become president—and I feared that the nature of the results might make it the last! The central finding from that project was one of the more daunting perspectives I'd had to deliver to any chief executive, telling him that his mission was akin to climbing Mt. Everest alone and without resources.

"You're right, Rich. The data showed that the public was not merely indifferent to the HIV/AIDS crisis; they were actually repulsed and hostile toward it."

"Exactly, they were repulsed and judgmental and all of that. And to cap it off, the Christian church at that time was absent without leave in the middle of the AIDS pandemic," he noted with sadness. "So one of the things we had to do at World Vision was cast a vision. I had to start with my employees because they were kind of where the evangelicals were in many ways. They were thinking, *We can't go there. A G-rated ministry like World Vision cannot get involved with an R-rated issue like that; it will backfire on us and stain our reputation.* That was the internal challenge. And then the external challenge was our donors, who were saying, 'Don't talk about this. I'm offended by it. I'm angered by it.' They did not want to face the fact that they were being judgmental or that they had attitudes about the issue that were inconsistent with their view of the role of World Vision.

"I had to paint a picture that changed the way people looked at and thought about HIV and AIDS. And that picture was designed to look at the world and present the reality of the AIDS crisis to our various publics in ways that changed their attitudes and views. So we started focusing on widows and orphans. The Bible has a wonderful verse about caring for widows and orphans in distress [James 1:27]. That's true religion, according to James. And, of course, widows and orphans were the innocent victims of AIDS. They had done nothing wrong. They just were at the receiving end of a terrible scourge. So we kind of went under the radar of the American public by talking about innocent widows and orphans.

"And we asked whether the Bible compels us to have compassion on people like this. Do they need to be loved and supported? Of course! So we identified things that we can do to make a difference. And then we started to talk about the scope of the pandemic. We began with Africa, where you've got seven countries where more than 20 percent of the people are HIV positive. They have teachers dying, farmers dying, government workers dying. It's destroying African society. Grandmothers are having to come out of their retirement in their seventies to care for ten, fifteen, twenty grandchildren."

There was a pause as Rich relived some of those difficult moments before he continued the story. "All of a sudden we were able to get to the heart of people. We knew that evangelical Christians have warm hearts underneath it all, but somehow we had to get to those hearts and get them to see HIV and AIDS from a completely different vantage point with a completely different lens. After making those inroads with people, I could then challenge them directly by asking, 'What is our responsibility? Where is the church in this? And what is our responsibility before God in the face of this global humanitarian crisis?'

"I went around the country speaking about this to audiences that I'm sure were quite skeptical and maybe a little surly at the beginning. But when I was done with the speech and we showed our video and we did our thing, people were flocking up to me in tears, saying, 'I've got to repent of my judgment, my judgmental attitudes. I never knew. I never understood this. How can I help?' People were able to see HIV and AIDS differently, and they began to understand how these things break the heart of God. That shift happened because of casting a vision. You know, it's really about worldview—offering a worldview that's compelling and truthful and motivating."

Everyone complimented Rich on a fitting story of making vision real—and for not backing down from overwhelming odds. Rich had done what every leader is supposed to do: in the words of one of our other speakers, Warren Bennis, a leader must do what is right.

Another lesson was evident from his story too: in the course of doing what is right, genuine leadership doesn't pander to public opinion and attitudes; it shapes it. The easy thing would have been for Rich to do what others before him had done: blanch at the magnitude of the challenge, recognize people's disinterest, and put his energy into something that was ready to roll. But his instinct and values told him that HIV and AIDS demanded attention, and he accepted the challenge. As a result, millions of lives had been and are still being saved thanks to their efforts.

"That's truly fantastic, but that's a nonprofit experience," someone respectfully noted. "It's not as easy to get people fired up about vision when it's about protecting shareholders who want to make as much money as possible off the work of the employees."

Whoa, there it was: the elephant in the room! The clash between money, motives, and morality. In essence, the argument was that cause-driven leaders have it easier than the business leaders of the world.

Rich smiled at that, as if he knew it was coming, and nonchalantly addressed the challenge.

"It is difficult, but I remember trying to do that in my corporate jobs, too. I was CEO of Lenox, the company that makes tableware, before coming to World Vision. And before that I was CEO of Parker Brothers, the company that makes games. When I first took over at Lenox, their market share in fine china was about 26 percent, and they claimed they were the number one china company in America. Noritake had a 28 percent market share, but the people at Lenox said, 'Yes, but that's not really fine china, that's Japanese china. Fine china is the European and American china.' That'd be like General Motors saying, 'Toyotas aren't really automobiles. Real automobiles are made by Americans.'"

Everyone had a good laugh at that—probably because every leader in the circle had had similar exchanges with the people they work with.

"So I had to change the worldview at Lenox to say, 'Wait a minute, Noritake is eating our lunch. And over the last five years our market share has decreased while theirs has increased.' You can't stick your head in the sand and say, 'Well, that's Japanese china.' One of the things I did to visually represent the situation was to create what we called the War Room. It was a conference room where on one wall we put the top fifty china patterns, by sales, in descending order. We actually bought a place setting of each one and we put them on the wall, ranked number one, number two, number three, number four, etc., so we could visualize Noritake's dominance. We did the same with flatware and stemware, as well. Then we held all of our product development meetings in that War Room so that all of the designers and all of the marketing people had to look at those other products every time we had a meeting. Well, five years later, Lenox had a market share of 45 percent and Noritake's had fallen to 16 percent. Obviously there was a lot of work that took place to get there, but it all started with creating a vision of reality and then a vision of what a better reality might be for Lenox."

Other leaders around the table began identifying examples they had been involved in, or knew of, where the vision process had been instrumental in a company's success. One of the most interesting companies to study has been Southwest Airlines. Having Colleen Barrett, who had just retired as president of the airline, in our group gave us a chance to get an insider's look at how Southwest had nudged their way into such a difficult industry—and redefined it at the same time. Colleen indicated that facing such overwhelming odds against success was one of the best things that ever happened to Southwest. It had, in essence, made their quest to launch their little regional airline a cause, similar in some respects to the uphill battle that Rich had faced at World Vision.

"When we started Southwest, we knew it was going to be very difficult to succeed. It was such a competitive industry, and we were trying to break in. We were the maverick, the black sheep, and most people wanted no part of us. The other guys at the time—the bad guys, the big, bad wolves—didn't think we stood a chance. They didn't think we would ever get off the ground, let alone fly. That's how Southwest became a cause for us. If they had left us alone, we probably would have been bankrupt in two years, and Herbert would be still practicing law today." She was referring to Herb Kelleher, the legendary founder of Southwest, who had been her boss and mentor. When Herb retired, Colleen was one of the people who stepped up to continue to lead the airline.

"But the more our competitors fought to keep us out of the air, the more competitive Herb became. They were arrogant and cocky, and we felt this was not right. When we began we were very small, maybe ten people. And we knew we wanted fighters, people who said, 'I'm going to fight for these guys because this is not fair.' I think it became the best David and Goliath story the business world has ever had. We had no money, so we couldn't buy ads, but we were on the front page of newspapers in Texas, where we started out, for three years running. From the day we got our certificate to the day we put our first airplane in the air, it was three and a half years. There were thirty-six legislative, legal, and administrative hearings involving all of these other competitors, based on charges they had leveled against us. And what did we have? One lawyer—Herb—who did it all out of his own pocket, and he was not a rich man. But he did it because he so believed in it.

"And the core culture of Southwest was formulated out of that struggle. We didn't say, 'This is going to be our culture,' but it evolved to the point that our culture included family, fun, and hard work. Herb wanted people to take our business very seriously, but not themselves. He valued a sense of humor, and I remember him telling our very first vice president of human resources to test potential employees for a sense of humor. She said, 'What am I going to do, put a whoopee cushion on the couch and see if they laugh?' But it's so easy to see if somebody has a sense of humor. And that has been a core value of Southwest."

The flow was interrupted for a minute or so as the other leaders said nice things about Southwest. Ever the killjoy, I wanted to get us back on track, so I deflated the lovefest with my next question.

"But how do you convert those values that Ken and Colleen and others of you are talking about into a lasting and healthy corporate culture?"

I thought I saw a few heads shake in disbelief as I killed the party spirit and pushed us back on task. Hey, a leader's not always going to be popular, right? Fortunately, Jimmy Blanchard—no relation to Ken, I later discovered—stepped into the gap to save me. Having led Synovus—a well-run, highly profitable financial services company—for years, Jimmy is a very gracious, intelligent man with great wisdom and experience.

"Repetition is how we do it," he explained, bringing the group back to focus. "At every gathering our flock hears the same sermon, over and over and over. We tell the same stories, emphasize the same concepts. We have a leadership meeting every Tuesday morning. It's not an information meeting, although we may dispense information. It's not a lecture, although from time to time we may lecture. It's not a classroom, although sometimes we try to educate. It is a cultural discussion or essay presented to reestablish who we are, what we stand for, what our core values are, and what our value chain is. That's what we believe works best in a company, rather than a bunch of rules. If your culture is strong and clear, it is communicated constantly, and there are no misgivings or ambiguities about what the culture is, then you are not going to get too many people too far afield.

"So I would say repetition is the number one thing. I have one story that I love to tell, and I have probably told it about four thousand times. Some of the people who work at Synovus have heard it all four thousand times, and it's kind of interesting because when I launch into telling that story, I see some of them kind of rolling their eyes, like, *Oh, man, here we go again.* But there's no misunderstanding about that story and what it means and what the lessons are. Take your vision and your values and put them in your printed material, put them in your orientations, put them in all of your leadership training at every level. But the main thing is that the key people, the folks that make the decisions in the company, should hear the CEO talking about these things all the time."

Having studied Synovus—they have received numerous awards as the best company to work for, as one of the innovators in their industry, and as a best-practices incubator, and they are known as a breeding ground for competent leaders—I was curious how they had managed to walk the line between profitability and pursuing core values that were so clearly faith based. The question didn't faze Jimmy in the least; he had obviously faced it many times before and had spent a lot of time thinking, discussing, and praying about that issue.

"You know, George, it is pretty clear to everybody that our value system is contained within the Judeo-Christian ethic. We are a public company, and I never felt like it was fair for me to stand up and preach. I never felt like it was my calling as the CEO of the company to take up an offering or have an altar call. In fact, I think that would be an abuse if they are required to come to my meeting. I can't impose my 'religious concepts' on these people, but I never had any constraints or pushbacks from imposing a culture that fundamentally is the Judeo-Christian ethic. Those values are about hard work, loyalty, brotherhood, and so forth. But it goes even a little deeper than that."

Jimmy paused and stared in acknowledgment at the other Blanchard in our group. "It's believing that the customer is right. It's a blessing to have these team members that have committed their career to our company. We are a custodian of their careers, fiduciaries. We have a responsibility because they have given us the best thing they've got—their work careers, their energy, and their time. We have to honor the trust that they put in us as a company.

"So ultimately, the value we have pushed and thrived upon is simple: we need to treat folks right. It doesn't matter who they are, or what church they grew up in, or what side of the tracks they came from, or the nature of their education. All people have worth, they are valuable, and they ought to be appreciated. We ought to be considerate and respectful of them. Those are the values that have become the meat of our corporate culture."

"We've had a similar experience at Wal-Mart," added Don Soderquist, without missing a beat. "Wal-Mart's values came from Judeo-Christian principles found in the Bible. Sam [Walton, Wal-Mart's founder] and I talked frequently about that, regarding what our foundation was and so forth. One of the primary principles found in the Bible is that we have respect for the individual. No matter what your beliefs may be, no matter what your background might be, no matter what color you are, the value is that you respect every single person because everyone is made in the image of God. That means that within the framework of Wal-Mart, regardless of what you may believe, no matter where you may have been raised, no matter what your religious preference might be, we respect you for who you are. That kind of environment is conducive to virtuous behavior. And that virtuous behavior is a result of the values that we have—just treating everybody like you want to be treated.

"Jim Collins was quoted a few years ago as saying that what distinguished Wal-Mart from the rest of the competition was its DNA. Wal-Mart has had a set of core values since the very beginning, and it all comes from a basic belief in the value of every single human being and that every person can make a contribution to the success of the company. They really believe that—it's not just hollow words. Wal-Mart is not perfect by any stretch of the imagination, but I think they more closely follow their words than any organization that I'm aware of."

Don's thoughts connected with something that was on Patrick Lencioni's mind.

"I agree. I think it's imperative to figure out what is core to the organization. You know it's a core value if you are willing to get punished for it, and if you see that, occasionally, your company takes it too far and it creates a problem but you are okay with that. Like Colleen said, one of Southwest

Airlines's core values is humor. And there's a great story to support that. Years ago, somebody wrote to Southwest and said, 'I'm a long-term customer, and I don't like the fact that you make jokes during the safety part of the flight.' Now most companies would write back to say, 'We value you as a customer, please trust that we care about your safety and we are good at that, but here's a free flight coupon and we will talk to the gate agents.' And then they would make a call and tell their people that the humor thing is good but they need to tone it down."

Patrick got a big smile on his face as he finished the story. "But not Southwest. No. They sent the customer a note that said, 'We will miss you.' That's when you know it's a core value. 'We will miss you.'" Now there were smiles all around the circle.

Having written bestsellers about dysfunctional companies, Patrick knew a lot about what makes or breaks a corporate culture. Someone asked him what kind of values his organization, the Table Group, has embraced in its effort to have a positive work environment.

"We talk about being humble, hungry, smart," he began with characteristic sincerity. "For instance, how can I create an environment where I will be the person I'm supposed to be? I hire people who are stronger than I am in humility, and who inspire me to work hard because that's who they are, and people who care about how others are feeling.

"All of that starts with my being brutally honest and vulnerable. People talk about humility and what that means, and the hard thing about humility is that when you think you have it, you probably don't, by definition. Vulnerability is when you realize you have made a mistake, or behaved poorly, or given in to temptations, and you call it out. I know that I'm a messy leader and a messy person. I'm a pretty intense and passionate person. And I know that if I'm not brutally honest about the times I make mistakes, I'll be miserable to work with, so I try to be vulnerable.

"For me, the guarantee that I will be humble is that I be vulnerable enough to be an open book with the people who work with me. I want people to tell me what their greatest weaknesses are and, as long as they are honest and real, knowing that they know it and are willing to say it is the thing that is probably most important for me."

Clearly, identifying a handful of core values and figuring out ways to hold people accountable for living in concert with those values is crucial. But I sensed a need to draw these people out a bit more regarding the development of a healthy culture. We seemed to be just touching the tip of that iceberg.

CHAPTER 4

CREATING
CULTURE

ALL THE TALK ABOUT vision and values naturally had led us to a conversation about corporate culture. If you define culture as all of the elements that comprise the environment in question—values, symbols, language, central beliefs, traditions, customs, and the like—then certainly every organization has a unique culture. And some of those cultures, of course, are more viable than others.

John Kotter, the esteemed professor of leadership from Harvard Business School, had joined our group, along with his similarly hallowed colleague from the University of Southern California, Warren Bennis. Who better to inform us about healthy cultures than these two icons of leadership wisdom? If clarifying and living consistently with your values bring about a healthy culture, what are some of the pitfalls that usher in an unhealthy culture?

"If a culture is inwardly focused, if it's bureaucratic, if it's political, if it doesn't pay attention to customers, if it's arrogant—we could come up with a long list of the attributes of unhealthy cultures," John said. "It's the stuff that slows you down, that doesn't draw on the talent of the organization, that doesn't deal with fundamentals—like making better products and services at good margins. If any of that has snuck its way into your culture, you've got to get it out.

"Most companies don't have perfect cultures, and leaders do need to work at that. But instinctively they usually do. It starts with modeling what's needed and then getting other people to do that, even if it's countercultural. The way culture develops is that a group of people does something in a certain way and it works. And if it works over a sufficiently long period of time, it seeps into the bloodstream of the organism. They don't do anything, it just happens. So what great leaders do is just that. If the culture isn't right, they get the group to act differently, get positive results, and if they just keep doing it for a while, it will start to seep into the bloodstream and replace the old stuff."

He shrugged as if it was so simple he couldn't believe he'd had to explain it to me. "I mean, that's it."

But it seemed to me that there were some important elements he had just included in that scenario. For instance, he had insinuated that the leader must analyze the culture with respect to the corporate values and identify the aspects that needed to be changed. Then the leader has to make sure his or her own behavior is consistent with the desired culture, and that people of influence within the organization pick up those values that are being modeled. And the leader must ensure that the group remains not only consistent in its practices, but persistent in maintaining those values as well.

To dig a bit deeper, I turned to John's fellow icon and asked Warren how he would go about creating a healthy culture.

"I would start with building a culture of candor," Warren responded. "It goes back to the transparency question. The cultures that are most toxic are those where nobody knows the truth or is talking about it. There's something to be said, George, about the legitimacy of doubt and being able, without scaring people, to talk about what we don't know about the current situation. Openness and transparency are important for the good of the organization. Toxic cultures are those where there usually isn't that degree of openness. And they can't be transparent about everything, but there are too many examples of companies failing where there's been a lack of transparency."

Thinking about the many organizations I have worked with over the years, I realized that few of the people in charge would have come out and admitted that theirs was an unhealthy culture. So I asked Warren how to deal with those situations; how do you help a leader immersed in his or her own toxicity to be able to see the conditions he or she has created or fostered for what they are?

"The indications of an unhealthy internal culture are easy to see if you look," he explained, echoing John's perspective. "Turnover, generally toxic relationships between people, not being able to attract good people, losing good people, and a lack of candor and directness in the organization. People must be able to speak truthfully to those with power."

Henry Cloud amplified Warren's point based on his own experiences.

"You know, one of the things that I've found about the cultures that have broken down is that they do not welcome the truth. They're sitting around in a meeting and somebody is sitting there saying, 'Gosh, I want to say A, B, or C, but I'm afraid.' I think safety is a big part of having a healthy culture."

Warren nodded and picked up that theme.

"Time Warner bought AOL when Jerry Levine was the chairman of Time Warner. It was a huge mistake, a bad acquisition. One of the people who worked for him, the number two guy, was very courageous in most cases. That was Dick Parsons, who's now the chairman. When I asked him, 'Dick, why didn't you try to talk Jerry out of this?' he said, 'There are certain things you don't talk to Jerry about.'"

So it sounds like it was a culture that lacked the openness and transparency that make for a healthy place. Can a toxic culture be changed, or is it too poisoned to recover?

Warren furrowed his brow as if I were missing the point. "Oh, no, it can be changed, but it's going to have to start from the top. There's an old saying that when a fish rots, it's the head of the fish that starts stinking first. It may not be *only* at the top where change is required, but it starts there because it kind of gels its way down. So it may take a major overhaul; becoming healthy sometimes takes serious surgery. That surgery means you get a new leader. Then comes the hard part: you've got to learn to work with the help and resources that are within the organization. You've got to identify people in the organization who share your goals. They've been overlooked and not taken seriously. They've not been part of the sickness, and you've got to discover who they are. And there are a lot of them who have been waiting for this change."

So you assess the environment and seek out the islands of strength and hope with whom you can work?

"That's right, work with the healthy ones. You've got to assume that people are good. And you've got to assume that there are good and healthy people there who want a healthy organization. If you come in and think, *Well, they're all a bunch of dissatisfied grumblers,* then you'll get nowhere."

I felt that I had grasped the basic concept, but I wondered how this might play out in an example from the real world. To clarify things, I asked him about the Jack Welch era at General Electric. Welch had created a dog-eat-dog culture that fared well for the bottom line but ravaged many individuals and torpedoed a number of careers. Did the public acclaim and the positive investment returns under Welch's command mean that GE had a healthy culture during the Welch years—despite the human carnage?

Warren's answer surprised me. "I think it did, because he was so explicit about his expectations and processes. Many huge companies like that probably have elements of toxicity. Welch coercively pushed people, and I think he lost some good people. But the beauty of what Welch did, to give him some credit, is that he was very clear. If you wanted to succeed with GE you knew this was the way it was going to be. You knew what you were coming up against in that culture. And there are people who thrive in that kind of setting."

I made a note to rethink some of my opinion of Jack Welch—and to keep in mind that a group's culture need not be and probably cannot be right for everyone. Warren correctly pointed out that Welch was simply pursuing a different set of values than those I would embrace, but by making those values clear, the former GE chairman could create a healthy culture even so.

While I was still trying to wrap my arms around that idea, I noticed John Townsend staring at me, as if the master psychologist were watching in fascination as the village idiot strained to comprehend a fundamental concept. Because John and I have a strong, playful relationship, I felt comfortable asking him—even in front of this august gathering of experts—for his input on the matter of creating a healthy culture.

"A healthy culture is one where people know they are around a leader who will lead, who will actually take the reins, create the vision, be ahead of the pack, make the hard decisions, care about the people, and protect the mission and the goals. The people know who the leader is.

"Secondly, it's a place where there's a team environment. People feel like there is cohesion and they are all valued parts of the whole—and that the bigger picture of us together is more important than any individual need. Because of that they have the idea that the more they work together and sometimes give up their individual desires, the more likely they are to create something much better. After all, that's what teams do.

"And thirdly, they create an environment where there's no such thing as a bad question. Because of that, people always question things; they're changing and challenging, and they're making mistakes—and all of that creates a very rich field of new ideas and new solutions to problems. I do a lot of leadership coaching, and one of the biggest things we see in the culture they are trying to develop is a place where people feel so safe and so much like they belong that they come up with ahas. They feel comfortable enough to ask, 'Why don't we try it this way?' a way that nobody has ever thought of, even though it might not work."

Maybe we were overlooking what it takes to create that kind of open, affirming culture. I pressed my colleagues to dive into that aspect of cultural development.

Henry Cloud took the lead. "You really need to come up with the vision of what you want the culture to be like, and you should involve people in that process. They're the ones who are going to live out that culture. A culture is sort of a two-way street; both leaders and others are going to have to live and breathe in it. So what you want to do is find out what's important to people in the culture. Then you have to have some values that are going to bring that vision to a reality and define behavior. Another thing that leaders need to do is build in some very structured training so that leaders under them know how to bring about that kind of culture on their own team. That means a leader has to spend time and money in developing people.

A healthy culture is one where people know they are around a leader who will lead, who will actually take the reins, create the vision, be ahead of the pack, make the hard decisions, care about the people, and protect the mission and the goals.

And good cultures are forever assessing their cultures. They do surveys, they have coaches, and they have consultants— all kinds of people coming in to find out anonymously how happy people are to be there, how challenged they feel, how exposed they feel to people leaving the team. You've got to be monitoring all of these things to find out where the disconnects are between what kind of culture the leader thinks he has and the kind he actually has."

Jon Gordon let loose next, building on Henry's statement that effective leaders provide people with a place where they can live and thrive. Jon's consulting with a variety of organizations supported that idea.

"The job of creating a culture is to develop an environment where people can perform at their highest potential. As a leader creating that culture, you want each person to stay positive, to utilize his or her gifts and strengths, and to contribute to the vision of the organization. So you create a culture where people can do their jobs in a positive manner. As a leader, it has to come from you. You can't delegate this one; this is your responsibility. You can't give it to HR. When Mike Smith took over as head coach of the Atlanta Falcons, a team that was a real mess, he was involved in every aspect of turning that culture around. He told me, 'I need to create a strong culture. Culture drives behavior, and behavior drives habits in an organization.'"

My longtime friend Ralph Winter was nodding his head in agreement. He knew what it must have been like for Coach Smith; Ralph produces blockbuster movies for the major studios. Over the past decade he has produced the films in the X-Men and Fantastic Four franchises, with some challenging one-offs in between.

"That's kind of like the movie business," Ralph shared. "You have to create that environment early on. You can't just turn it on fifty days in. Nobody believes it is sincere at that point. In our case, we consciously try to establish a culture in our preproduction phase, before we get on the set and then move to postproduction. We seek a culture that upholds having fun, making the experience enjoyable, making it interesting to come to work, and having an open environment where people aren't criticized for their ideas but are complimented on them and encouraged to provide input." He had just returned from months on the set of an upcoming megarelease, where he had overseen the spending of more than $100 million over the course of just a few months, directing the activity of hundreds of cast and crew with the hope of creating a memorable and beloved film.

"No matter how well conceived it is, though, the culture only becomes real when your people see it backed up—when others see their ideas being given careful consideration, and they are not being criticized for bringing up new ideas."

"One way to get a healthy culture is to hire healthy people," offered Miles McPherson, drawing on his experience of leading a large church as well as several growing nonprofit ventures. "You have to get people who are emotionally healthy. You cannot ask immature people to be mature; they just can't do it. When you hire immature or unhealthy people, they're going to nurture an unhealthy culture and then blame you for it. And honestly, part of the fault is yours because you hired them in the first place.

"In addition," he continued, "you didn't boldly and courageously hold them accountable for what was right. It is important to clarify all of the words you use to define your culture. Since one of our initiatives for this year is to cultivate a loving, people-first culture, we must first define *culture*. Then we must define what *loving* and *people-first* mean—and what they do not mean. We have to define the words and make sure everyone buys into those definitions and the expectations that come with them."

General Bob Dees, who had served on the Joint Chiefs of Staff as well as various overseas assignments in the army, added to Miles's words about the importance of definitions and language.

"Sometimes culture happens innately. But when you look closely at high-performing organizations, one of the things you see is that they develop their own metalanguage. It becomes tribal wisdom and culture. In the military, it's a lot of the acronyms or shared experiences. For instance, in the army and marines, the word *hoo-ahh* is a word used a hundred different ways. It can mean you're happy, sad, having a good day—it all depends on the inflection of the voice. But it's part of the metalanguage that's endearing and has a lot of meaning in that particular tribal culture."

"You know, Steve Wynn was on TV last week," came the deep, deliberate voice of Kirbyjon Caldwell. He had left a successful Wall Street career a couple of decades ago to pioneer entrepreneurial ministry ventures in an economically depressed section of Houston, including a large church of nationwide influence. He was referring to a show featuring the brash and aggressive owner of several Las Vegas casinos.

"It was very interesting. He has opened up a brand-new hotel in Las Vegas and is going to hire five thousand new people to staff it. He said the greatest thing that a businessperson can do right now is to make certain he or she is taking care of his or her employees. In today's economy, communication is a leader's most important asset. He said, 'I communicate with my employees weekly. All of them.' So when you are talking about establishing the type of culture you want, you must make certain the employees know what you expect, know what the vision is, and know what it takes to pursue that vision, and you need to make sure they have what they need in order to do what you are asking them to do."

It was getting close to my time to return to the big stage and transition from our current speakers to the next group. But before I headed toward the door leading to the stage, Ken Melrose spoke up again, talking about his experience of redirecting Toro from its old-school, hierarchical model to a more open, collaborative culture.

"We had to transform our culture from a top-down decision-making process to a bottom-up process. One of the things that we did to try to change the culture was ask Ken Blanchard to help us change this very negative organization. Remember, we almost went bankrupt in the early '80s, and everyone was focusing on the problem. Ken came in and said, 'You've got to catch people doing things right.'

"So we had a big wave of trying to focus on the positives, highlight things that turned out well, recognize the people who were making something good happen. After Ken's advice, I had a staff meeting and told all the people who reported to me, 'The first thing we're going to talk about, in each of your areas, is what good things happened in the last week.' The first time we did this there was a lot of silence. No one said anything. I encouraged them to speak up. 'Anyone, volunteer, just blurt it out. What went well in your group or your division last week?' Still, nobody said anything. I looked at my watch and I said, 'Okay, meeting's over.' I got up and walked out of the room.

"And the following week the same thing happened. I said, 'Okay, if we can't talk about what you want to talk about, you're the problem until you can talk about catching somebody in your division doing something right. Meeting's over.' So I think the staff said, 'Gee, this guy is serious. We're not getting anything done. We're not getting decisions made. We're not getting the input we need. We've got to find something good going on in our groups.' So they went back to their departmental staff meetings and said, 'Hey, tell me something good that's happening here so I can take it back to Ken's staff meeting.' So everyone in the organization started looking for good things. And when good things happened, they reported it. Stories began to emerge. The programmer who stayed at Toro all weekend to fix a problem, for example. And we'd go to that person and say, 'Attaboy! Why don't you take your wife to dinner, on us, because you did such a great job.' Or sometimes we'd call a meeting to recognize that victory; everyone would get a piece of pie and would celebrate this person or that team's good work.

"Sure enough, the whole organization began to realize, 'Hey, things are good here. We may be going bankrupt, but things are really good here.' And it was that attitude shift that made such a difference. But it was driving down this culture change that transformed the organization. It happened intentionally. We were overtly trying to change the way we made decisions, the way we treated each other, what the Toro family was all about. We had a lot of pushback. To get people to buy into this we eventually said, 'We have people values and performance values. For the performance values, your supervisor's going to rate you. But for your people values, like catching people doing something right, you're going to get rated by the people who work for you, on a confidential basis.' We had six people values, things like communicating with people, being open to new ideas, valuing one another, being team-oriented, and so forth.

"Some of our managers were getting really low scores and no bonuses, and they left. And we figured that was good for them to leave and good for us, because they weren't on board with the culture we were building. We weeded out a lot of people who refused to be part of the new way. They'd say, 'That's not what I was taught in business school. I was taught to be strong and dominant and powerful and make the big decisions.' And we said, 'Sorry, that's not part of our culture here.' So that transition was very overt, and it took a lot of time, but gradually we started rebuilding trust."

As I headed for the door, struck by the significance of culture, I heard Laurie Beth Jones affirm Ken's story. "Culture is a socially transmitted way of practices. It's not about what's written down. Policy and procedure manuals are worth nothing. Leaders have to model the culture on a day-by-day basis or it will never take root."

CHAPTER 5

DEVELOPING LEADERS

I RETURNED FROM THE STAGE to the greenroom, having dismissed the crowd for the midmorning break. After a brief huddle with the production team to review how things were going and make a few minor adjustments to our process, I was back with all of the speakers, who were busy interacting with each other. Things were going very smoothly so far.

After getting a bottle of water and a banana, I wedged into one of the groups and listened in. They seemed to be discussing the process of determining who has leadership potential.

"Leader selection is critical. You do your best to identify those who are leaders. Sometimes you're right, sometimes you're wrong," admitted Bob Dees, thinking back on his years in the army and his subsequent stint as an executive at Microsoft. "But I think we often have it out of balance in terms of leader selection and leader development. We need to place greater priority on leader selection. Often, when we select leaders, we spend a brief time assessing their true capabilities and figuring out what's the right seat on the bus for them, but then spend a lot of time trying to turn a Chevy into a Cadillac after we've put them in a position they're not well suited for. We really have to figure out what is the best place for each leader, based on his or her abilities, motivations, and all that. We also have to place people in positions in such a way that they're not in a box so that if we have to shift things around, they're thrilled by it rather than disappointed or threatened."

No doubt about it, selecting and growing leaders is an art. The difficulty of getting it right was confirmed by Tony Dungy. "That's the trial-and-error process," agreed the respected coach, "but I think you try to bring out the best in everyone, and then you see which people have those natural leadership skills, the ones whom other players watch and gravitate toward. You pick those guys out pretty quickly and say, 'Hey, I need you to be on board with me, number one, but I have seen some other skills in you, too.' And then you encourage them to become leaders."

The comments from Bob and Tony helped me to realize that it's not often that someone taps you on the shoulder and acknowledges a leadership gift. My research had shown that when you seek out raw talent to nurture into leaders, you search for two primary elements: a sense of calling to lead and the kind of solid, enviable character that enables the leader to make appropriate choices and to attract people by virtue of who he or she is deep inside. Competencies are the third element that makes someone a genuine leader, but skills can be taught and refined, whereas calling and character are part of a leader's innate package. With this team of leaders gathered, I wondered aloud what they felt someone should look for as a potential mentor to the next generation of leaders.

Selecting and growing leaders is an art.

"It helps to be wise more than smart, smart more than dumb, and persistent more than anything else," suggested Newt Gingrich matter-of-factly. "If you're persistent, wise, and smart, then you probably get Lincoln.

Wisdom beats being the smartest. That's the great problem Bill Clinton had. Clinton is tremendously smart; he just has the least wisdom of a senior leader I've ever seen."

Oh boy. Now we had the makings of a heated debate among a group of people who, by definition, don't shy away from conflict. Inevitably, someone noted that President Clinton had left behind a good track record of policy accomplishments and economic stability, and asked Newt why he had such a dour assessment of the abilities of the former president.

"Because he's existential. His entire life is spent on the now. The first time I ever saw him in the cabinet, I said, 'This is FDR without polio.' He is the most skillful politician of his generation, but he has none of the iron that polio drove into FDR. He's a brilliant politician."

Fortunately, that did not set off a range war based on the divergent political perspectives in the room. I was most intrigued by the fact that Newt had pointed out that wisdom and persistence are essential qualities in a leader. Colleen Barrett deftly sidestepped the political land mine and added a new twist on the search for future leaders.

"I think you can identify leaders by asking people questions—not specific questions, but just questions about their life. You can find out if they have natural leadership skills, whether you ask them about their school, life experiences, charitable causes, or community efforts. What I try to do is get a feel for the person's philosophy of life. It's not a right or wrong thing, but I will ask people to tell me about a time when they handled conflict. I will ask people, 'How did you use a sense of humor to diffuse a bad situation?'"

What an interesting statement. Colleen had connected her company's core values—in this case, having a good sense of humor—to her search for someone who had leadership potential and could express that potential in harmony with the organization's cherished values. I wondered aloud if these leaders did much in terms of trying to determine if a person has been called to lead.

"Let me tell you a funny story," said Ken Blanchard, who has to be one of the best parable tellers I've ever met. "I was doing a program in

Canada for the Young Presidents' Organization with Henry Blackaby. We were sitting there on stools and they were asking questions. And one of the questions that came up was, 'What do you think about the Gallup research that says you should first find out your strengths and then that will tell you what a good job fit would be?'"

I'd heard several of the leaders present raise this very matter—the StrengthsFinder process—and had only heard complimentary things about that research and the tools that emanated from it. Ken continued his story. "And Henry, in his beautiful way, said, 'It's an interesting theory. It's just not sound biblically. You name one person whom the Lord called who was qualified. They all complained, whether it was Abraham or Moses or Mary. The Lord doesn't call the qualified, the Lord qualifies the called.'

"So I asked Henry, 'Well, what does it mean to be called?' He said, 'It means to be humbled and to be open to learn.' Isn't that interesting? Suppose you have an opportunity to lead but it's not in your strength area. What are you going to do? Well, if you're called to do it, you ought to do it, but then you should be humble enough to say to people, 'I'm going to need your help.'

"The timing of Henry's comment was really great, because we had made a mistake in appointing somebody as the president of our company. It was a woman with great energy and a lot of skills, but when she became president she became an animal. She attacked our people and all that kind of thing. So right after that our family had to regroup, because my wife and I and our two kids and my wife's brother run the company. But none of us wanted to be president at that particular time, so we had to do some reorganizing. They asked my daughter to take over sales. We've got sixty salespeople. The only experience Debbie had ever had in sales was working for Nordstrom's one summer when she was in college. So you would think, 'Yikes! They're putting Debbie in as vice president of sales. How ridiculous is that?'

"So what did Debbie do? She called a meeting of all the salespeople and said, 'If I told you I know what I'm doing in this job, we could all have a great laugh. But the one advantage is that I'm a Blanchard and what I'm going to do is travel all over the country to meet with you and find out what you need and what we can do to help you be more effective. I think I can carry that ball.' Well, nobody complained at all. So the idea of being called and then being humble and open to learning turned out to be a wonderful concept."

It was a great story, but I was not yet convinced that such openness enables a person to rise up and become an effective leader. I took on the role of the skeptic.

"I hear you, Ken. But is it really that simple? Everyone in this room has extensive education and experience, and it seems perhaps too simplistic to believe that all you need is someone who wants to lead and is open to growing. Newt talked about a few qualities that you need to look for. Don't we need to somehow screen people a little more carefully instead of training them just because they showed up?"

John Townsend came to Ken's aid. "You have to convince people that they should learn to lead and then they should lead. They should develop whatever skills they have and then use those skills. There is no leadership development process that occurs overnight. It's going to take time; it gradually happens. But keep in mind that if the person really doesn't see the point of developing the skills or doesn't want to use them, then it's not going to happen. So I think a very important up-front piece is to help the people who want to lead and are willing to work at it. I'm not convinced that the first thing to do is to drag in people who don't know much about leadership or don't know much about why it applies to them.

"Once someone has internalized that, you don't have to just shove leadership training down their throats. They'll go out and look for it—jobs that help develop them and other kinds of growth experiences. I'm beginning to think that may be the biggest single key in all of this. There are plenty of opportunities out there that are real opportunities—both on the job and off the job—to test, and try, and learn from your successes and mistakes."

Okay, so my skeptic's approach hadn't panned out too well; John had largely reinforced Ken's point of view. Point made. But I was still wondering how to identify genuine leaders who are worth investing in. Certainly it takes more than wisdom, intelligence, and perseverance. It must demand more than an open mind and a willingness to lead. So with John Kotter standing among us, I asked him for his thoughts on the issue. This was the guy who had trained hundreds of CEOs and other top-notch executives. How do we figure out who is really a leader?

"I've heard that question often over the years. Let me flip it around. Why wouldn't you know?" John laughed at this turning of the tables. "I think that's a more honest question. Maybe because you never look at them or you never talk to their subordinates? Let's turn it around the other way. If you pay any attention to your people and watch them with their own subordinates and even talk to their subordinates—not necessarily by asking, 'How good a leader is he?' but by listening to the way he or she talks about the leader—wouldn't you know? I don't think it's that mysterious."

"John, it sounds to me as if you're saying that leaders know their own kind—with a little bit of awareness and effort they can see it, sense it, and understand that capacity in others. And conversely, if you're not a leader, you wouldn't know what you're looking for anyway."

"Correct," he said, nodding at me. "I make speeches around the world, usually to a company's senior management. Beforehand we will create a video clip about a really good leader from the country I'll be speaking in. Let's say I don't have an example from that country. What will I do?

"First, I will e-mail the person who invited me and ask him or her to ask around to find out what CEOs in that country are good leaders. Now what did that take me, maybe six seconds to type? Then I get an e-mail back with three names. Next, I e-mail back and ask the person to find people who know these three CEOs well. Include one or several subordinates, maybe a customer or two, but give me six people who know them, and here's a good way to do it. You put a little questionnaire in front of them that takes them all of thirty seconds to fill out. You put the guy's name on it who they know very well and ask them how good that person is on six or seven different kinds of actions ranked on a scale of 0 to 10. How good of a finance guy is he? How good of an entrepreneur is he? How good of a manager is he? How good of a salesman is he? How good of a leader is he? How good of a manufacturing manager is he? You kind of slip the leadership factor in there. So she does this routine and comes back with information, and one of the people rates, across the six samples, 9.5 on leadership. And I go get a video of him on the Internet, watch it for four minutes to see if the 9.5 seems reasonable. As I expected, it probably is a good number. And so I figured out who a good leader is based on a total time investment of about five minutes. People can't figure out who has got leadership potential? That's a mystery to me." We all laughed at how simple John had made something that often seems complex.

I was hoping that these experts would similarly simplify the process of leadership development. I plunged forward with a series of questions on this front. Henry Cloud had been watching with amusement and entered the fray.

"Remember that any closed system deteriorates over time. That's the law of entropy. But the way you reverse a closed system is by introducing two things: a new energy source and a template to organize that energy. So if you take a potential or new leader and you want him or her to become more ordered over time toward leadership and not more disordered, then you've got to do both of those; you've got to make sure that that leader is an open system where you are pouring in two things.

"The energy can be in the form of support, inspiration, encouragement, motivation, pushing, driving, lighting a fire under them, giving new experiences that add heat to the fire.

"But then you also need a template. Just like DNA: when your body eats broccoli, that's fuel and energy, but your brain and your DNA organize that to become a particular kind of a bone. An organization really needs a structured leadership template, which is what they have decided leaders in the organization must know, and how they must behave, and what they must do in order to accomplish what they're trying to do.

"Just as spiritual formation is forming a character in the ways of God, leadership formation is forming the makeup of leaders in the ways of a company and the ways that they want to see their leaders performing. To do that you create experiences that give the leaders bite-size spheres in which they can fail, kind of like a dress rehearsal before the performance or practice before the big game. You want to put people in actual situations where they use their gifts and they go out and try things, where the world's not going to blow up if they don't get it right because they're learning. But that only helps if you've got feedback mechanisms and coaches and models to help them in the process.

"So I'm a real strong believer in the idea that leaders are built in part by modeling. They really learn from people who are coaching them. And I always try to coach my leaders to become coaches. Leadership development, in some form or fashion, is always about leaders being coaches."

But exactly how does that coaching happen? What does it look like? Is it formal or informal? Scheduled or spontaneous? Based on a checklist of qualities to promote or built around the needs of the moment? Inquiring minds want to know!

John Kotter took the floor again, sharing some of his many years of experience in how a leader is formed. "I personally think education can play a big role in the transfer of information, but books do that too—and books are much more efficient," the professor noted. "I can read them in my living room, but I can't take your class in my living room. And books are cheaper. As long as you define education as information transfer, frankly books are the way to do it. So what is the unique role of face to face?" John asked rhetorically. "It not only passes on information but it can grab attention. All great instructors throughout history have not only known their subject matter but they've been inspirational. They don't have to have a big, extroverted personality; they don't have to be charismatic. But I think all great instructors are inspirational around their topic. People walk out not only with more knowledge, but wanting to learn more, excited about it. Their level of passion around that topic goes up. With all of that, much more happens beyond just taking a course. On average, books aren't nearly as inspiring as a good classroom setting can be."

A few comments were made reinforcing the value of an inspiring teacher. Some of the leaders in the room had grown through classes they had taken with Professors Kotter, Bennis, and Blanchard, and had undoubtedly been inspired by those great teachers. Jimmy Blanchard affirmed the place of both books and classroom-style training.

"I have been reading all the books I can, and I love the opportunities to go to any kind of leadership training. We made a decision twenty-five years ago that we might make some mistakes, and some big ole alligators might grab us and take us under, but putting people in jobs that they are not prepared for because we have not invested in their training is one mistake we are not going to make. And so we have had basic leadership, high-level leadership, and mid-supervisory leadership; every kind of leadership training you could have. In 1999, *Fortune* named us the best place in America to work. I'm not going to sit here and pretend we really are the best place, but we were flattered with the recognition, and it validated to us that training and preparing leaders, teaching them the basics, and trying to enthuse them to seek their own highest level of leadership was a good approach and a good investment in a corporate environment.

"It has certainly paid off. One thing we learned is that developing leaders is probably the most appreciated benefit in the company. When current or would-be leaders realize that you are investing in their growth, it's more important to them than money. It's more important, in my opinion, than a supervisor taking personal interest in their person and encouraging them along the way in their career, although that is probably second. So we learned that it is an incredibly important investment, not only for the company, but in the minds of the individuals who are participating.

"By the way, we found that our best leaders always just couldn't wait to get to the next training program because they knew they were going to get something good out of it. The worst of our supervisors—I won't call them leaders—would gripe and grouse and complain. 'I don't have time.' 'How do they expect me to do my job and take two days off for leadership training?' 'How many times do I have to learn about Maslow's triangle?'

These were the people who said, 'I don't really need this; I'm already a good leader.' And they were the worst. So it's been a pretty good little test for us. When you look at people who are eager to learn more, you can bet they are on the right track. And when you talk to people who just don't want anymore instruction, then they have pretty much hit the wall. They are done."

Someone asked Jimmy what Synovus does to train leaders in-house.

"The most successful training that we have had for the really top-level folks is similar to an executive MBA program. We believe that the courses we have developed are as good as any of the six-week programs that so many top-level guys have done. Ours is high level, with all kinds of participatory programs that you get involved in and simulated business experiences. But we make sure we don't leave out basic conceptual stuff even at the top-level training. You just cannot overdo basic conceptual training."

Warren Bennis indicated his admiration for such in-house programs but pointed out an unstated principle that was fundamental to what Synovus and other companies are doing to elevate their leaders.

"I think the most important and difficult thing is to create a culture in the organization where leadership is really important. It's important for people in the company to realize that this is a growth-oriented company, and the biggest thing we have to grow here is you, because it's you who will make this company better and better by your own growth. So there are some measures to put in place. What percentage of the payroll goes into leadership development? What kinds of formal training do they do? To what extent do they reward leadership? Do they have a directory of good mentors? So I would think making a culture aware of the significance of developing leaders is valuable. The main things are the visible efforts, like the percentage of payroll designated for training, or the number of opportunities they give people to attend conferences on the topic, or that they reimburse for classes taken at a university. Intel has done this for years. Andy Grove and Gordon Moore used to teach that. PepsiCo is another good example. For a long time their leaders have been very conscious of pushing leadership training, and I think they've done pretty well. Roger Enrico, their former CEO, was a good example of a leader consistently tutoring a group of people inside the organization."

There we were again, back at the idea of creating a particular kind of culture—in this case, one that affirms and supports good leadership. And we had been given some practical examples of how it works: books, classes, mentoring, performance rewards, and the like. A couple of people picked up on the comments that both Jimmy and Warren had made about in-house coaching and role modeling as necessary components.

"Role modeling is such a powerful way to develop certain kinds of behaviors," John Kotter reminded us, coming back to the admonitions Henry Cloud had given us a few minutes ago. "If you keep people by you all the time who need to learn something about leadership, then by definition the amount of time you're spending, in a sense, teaching other people your leadership approach is 100 percent."

Kirbyjon Caldwell climbed on that bandwagon. "I'm not the kind of leader who will hold your hand and sit down with you once or twice a week and go over stuff. The way I mentor people is by having them watch me and ask questions. It is more of a 360-degree learning experience."

"So if I'm hearing this right, Kirbyjon, with your style of leadership it's important for you to be accessible to people, to be visible, and perhaps even vulnerable?"

Kirbyjon gave me the eye. "Yeah, that's right. Accessible, visible, vulnerable. I like that." He turned to the person next to him and said mockingly under his breath, "I need to write that down. Accessible, visible, and vulnerable." We all laughed as he clapped me on the back.

It turned out that Kirbyjon was not alone in his method of coaching leaders. "When I travel, I always bring somebody with me. I never go to an event or a client without a person from my staff," said Patrick Lencioni. "That's my time to be with them, and, honestly, I think that's when I do my coaching and my leadership evaluating. When I come back from a trip, I will have spent four hours on a plane, plus other time with this person, and then four hours back. Goodness gracious, that's more time than an hour spent one-on-one. And it's good time, too, because we are talking about life."

Patrick's energy had sparked heightened interest in our conversation. And people's attention multipled as Lou Holtz joined in. Coach doesn't speak much—he's a classic "speak when you're spoken to" kind of guy—but when he does speak, I've learned that you're a fool not to listen.

"These days I get hundreds of letters from athletes thanking me or saying they accomplished this or that and just wanted to share it with me," he said softly, his eyes perhaps glistening a bit. "When we had many of our former Notre Dame football players come back, I used to say to them that I didn't coach football, I taught life. The same things that make you successful in football will enable you to be successful in life. With our players, I'd say to them, 'I go all over the world speaking. Companies want me to come and speak, and they're willing to pay me a huge sum of money to speak to them. And I speak to you for free, and you don't even take notes.'" He smiled that warm, friendly smile of his. "Yeah, I'd ride them about that all the time. And they laugh about it now and say, 'We wish we had taken notes.' You don't always get through to all of them. Sometimes they acquiesce to your demands because you're in charge; some do so because they realize you aren't going to compromise and give in to their standards. But it's after they're gone that you have to look in the mirror and say, 'I think I did the best I could for that individual.'"

Laurie Beth Jones brought up an important caveat about the process. Her research had led to a book—in fact, an entire training process—in which she associates every person to one (or a combination) of the four elements (wind, earth, water, fire), recognizing the differences in how people are wired and how that wiring affects execution. "But remember, you cannot treat everybody the same way and get the same results. That's where the science of leadership comes in. When you realize that you are dealing with somebody who is not going to be moved by sentiment, then you start giving them facts and time to process. If you are dealing with people who are very relational, you better start showing them how this is going to improve their relationships and how you are thinking about people in whatever decision you are making."

Then she went back to something that Kirbyjon and others had been emphasizing. "An almost universally neglected commitment is making it a primary practice of the leadership team to develop leaders internally. That requires having a personal mentorship program and recognizing that everyone's role is developing leaders for the next generation. It's one of their most important roles.

"That is what Jesus did, and I think He was very aware of what motivated His individuals. He really cultivated and developed the workers who were going to carry on the work after He left. You need to give daily examples and reward, in the moment, the behaviors you want to see multiplied. Jesus showed them that even if you give a drink of water to someone who is thirsty, you will be rewarded. That's a cultural establishment principle. It's not just about the big things, it's also about the little things. Showing them that this is what God is looking for in terms of behaviors, this is what will be rewarded—this and this, but not that. A good leader shows people what a good day looks like."

Bob Dees was totally on board with Laurie Beth's ideas and seized the opening to add on a complementary experience he'd had.

"I recall an incident when I was a cadet at West Point. I was in Germany in a training environment and we didn't have any training aids, like Power-Point or projectors. But I always thought it was a sin to bore the troops when you were training them, so I asked my platoon sergeant for some chalk and an armored personnel carrier. He got them, and we used the side of the carrier as a blackboard. I recognized you can talk to the troops all day long, but working in pictures and simple concepts is far more powerful. So I started imparting vision to them regarding where, how, and why in very simple terms. As a developing leader myself, I began to appreciate the power of simplicity, the power of figuring out the vocabulary of the people you're talking to and the necessity of selling the solution ahead of time, and the power of empowerment. When you sell the solution, the essence of that is convincing them that they thought of it and they are understood and respected as a member of the group that will get to the desired destination."

Bob's experience reminded me of the axiom that it's amazing how much a leader can get done if he doesn't care who gets the credit. Overall, then, my mentors seemed to agree that training leaders is critical, the process must be multifaceted, and it will probably only work if you have the right people involved—people who want to lead, want to learn, and realize that they have a lot of room for growth.

It's amazing how much a leader can get done if he doesn't care who gets the credit.

Sadly, the break time was over and I had to run out to the main stage to corral everyone back to the auditorium. We had another great session about to start, and people needed to get back in their seats. And I was already thinking about the next set of questions I wanted to pose to our leadership experts.

CHAPTER 6

HIRING THE
RIGHT PEOPLE

BY NOW, THE CONFERENCE had developed a good rhythm and was advancing smoothly. Our speakers were really delivering the goods, and in return they were consistently showered with warmth and appreciation from the audience. Meanwhile, the greenroom had become an interesting place for the speakers to hang out when they were not onstage or doing a workshop. The leaders assembled in the room seemed comfortable either joining our little brainstorming groups or peeling off for a while to get some private time.

Redirecting my thoughts from the isolation of the main stage to the camaraderie and dialogue in the greenroom, I centered on the reality that leadership is impossible without vision, and while a leader is both defined and limited by his or her character and competencies, leadership is ultimately a people game. Our previous discussion about identifying potential leaders and then determining how to develop their leadership capacity raised some bigger questions about working with people. After all, the pursuit of the vision is a shared experience; no leader fulfills the vision alone. So the process of surrounding yourself with the right people—hiring, evaluating, and firing—became my launching point. Who do you hire? How do you make that decision? What is the most efficient process? I wanted to know what these leaders had learned about this make-or-break aspect of pursuing the vision.

Colleen Barrett was standing there sipping from her cup. She struck me as the ultimate people person—interested in others, a good listener, a humble spirit, and open to helping however she could. She was happy to share her views about hiring people at Southwest.

"We are almost religious about hiring. We hire their attitude and then we train for skill. We want to win by being the best customer service–oriented company, so we look for caring, fun-loving, spirited people who want to deliver customer service. We tell our applicants, 'Before you can go on the payroll, you must understand that we are in the customer service business. We just happen to provide airline transportation.'"

That was a good start—looking for a good attitude, one that fits with the core values of the organization. But what else helps an organization to know if a candidate will be a good fit for a leadership role? I posed that as a general question to those gathered around the newly replenished munchies.

"I tell people it's important to get to know someone's character," was John Townsend's advice. "Choosing someone cannot be based on a single event. What I mean by that is you should never hire somebody because of one interview or one set of references or a 360-degree review or whatever, because character comes only out of a process. However you do this, don't rely upon a snapshot, because anybody can look good in a snapshot. You need to get and review the entire videotape. Look at people over time. Look at them under stress. If you can, meet their families and talk to their friends."

Someone commented that even when you do all those things you can still get burned. John acknowledged that and provided an additional step.

"If possible, hire someone on a probationary basis and watch what happens when he or she deals with difficult situations. Then you'll find out if that person is a fit. The really good, successful, big organizations in America always have some type of long probationary period where they can see a person over the seasons of time, both the good times and the bad."

That idea sparked a comment from Lou Taylor. The staff at the thriving management agency she founded and deftly leads makes significant life-charting decisions with and on behalf of a wide range of high-profile celebrities. Because of that, her organization requires employees with a diverse set of skills.

"The thing that works the best for me is finding people for my organization whom I've worked with in another capacity or whom the people I work with know personally."

I was a bit surprised by that strategy, because it seemed as if it would limit the field of possible candidates for any given position she was trying to fill. Lou reminded me that like most of the people in the room, she is connected to many people whom she knows and trusts, thus making the field of possibilities rather large and fertile. But she also pointed out that the reason for restricting her search to "known commodities" was quite practical.

"Their moral constitution and their ability to make appropriate decisions are crucial to me," Lou emphasized. "We deal with too much money and too many high-profile people not to have somebody who is absolutely grounded." Then she affirmed John's recommendation of using a probation period with all new hires. "I tell them that coming in to the job, and let them know that they're going to have 60 to 120 days—whatever we agree upon—to show me who they are. I have learned not to feel guilty anymore if someone is not the right person. If they aren't right for us, I don't keep them. That's something I grew into because for a long time I wanted to give everyone the chance to make it. I wanted to *make* it work, no matter what. But now, if they're not in the groove by day sixty, or however long we had agreed to, I just don't keep them. I simply tell them, 'It's just not working out.' Everybody comes to us on a trial basis."

If you've ever been on the set of a blockbuster movie as it is being filmed, you know the complexity of the task and the number of specialists running around the soundstages. Ralph Winter, thinking about his vast experience hiring numerous leaders and executives for the dozens of movies and television shows he has produced, nodded in agreement, but wanted to add a caveat.

"But you have to be careful about hiring friends, because it doesn't always work out. And as a Christian, particularly with Christian friends, you have to be careful that you don't make it too spiritual. Because then when they aren't meeting the performance goals, you have to make a judgment call. On the one hand, you have somebody who wants to connect with you relationally, and on the other, you're responsible for producing results. I feel like this is where you get manipulated sometimes. It's easy to get those dimensions confused, and it can be difficult to separate those out in a business environment.

"For me, the best approach in working with Christian people I know has been to lead with business matters first," Ralph concluded pensively. "You have got to be careful about that. I think it is possible to care about them individually, but then when the hard times come you may have a time when you have to separate, either by firing them or letting them leave if they want to go. In some ways you have to prepare for that in the beginning. That's what contracts are about; contracts are what you turn to if it doesn't go well, and that defines how you separate. I have tried hard to distinguish between my relationship with an employee or a fellow worker as a believer and as a business partner, so we don't get the two confused. I am trying to run the business and operate with a business relationship. They have to understand that on a relational basis, I love them as brothers or sisters in Christ, but they also need to know that we can't work together if they are not meeting the performance evaluations of what we agreed they would do."

At this point, Mike Huckabee entered the dialogue, having had to figure out the balance of faith and leadership in both governmental and ministry settings.

"You know, you have to care about them because they're human beings, and you have to recognize that their personal lives affect their performance. That's just the Golden Rule. But you also need to recognize that you have been hired to get a certain job done, and when this person becomes unable to help you with that job, then you have to separate the task from the person. The best way to do that is to have people on your team in a caretaking role so you are getting reports that allow you, if necessary, to move that person out of the way. And that's hard, it's very hard; but in the long term, it's best not only for the organization, but best for the person.

"If you have somebody who can't function in his or her job for whatever reason, you do that person a greater service by moving him or her out. As the leader I need to spare you the humiliation and embarrassment and free you to do something you can do well. It's really in the best interest of that person. You don't want to put people in jobs they can't handle, because that forces them to fail and become demoralized. It all goes back to treating others like you want to be treated. You don't put people in a situation where they are destined for failure."

Ralph and Lou concurred with Mike that every case is a bit different and has to be handled carefully, without basing hiring decisions on assumptions and rigid rules. The importance of being cautious and doing it right was underscored by John's longtime colleague Henry Cloud.

"The research says that if you don't have the right person doing the right thing, then it's going to take you a long time, a lot of effort, and a lot of resources to get rid of that person. And then you've got to start all over and you've lost all that time, the opportunity cost, etc. So this is huge. And here's the problem." Henry paused to take a bite from the sandwich he was holding. Because people issues are so critical to a leader's success, everyone waited patiently to hear what was coming next.

"The problem is that leaders, by definition, oftentimes have the organizational leverage, capacity, resources, and power to fall in love with a psycho." Everyone laughed at Henry's blunt statement of a reality we have all experienced. "We see it every day. Leaders get an agenda, they go out there and interact with people, and the last person they meet is the world's greatest expert. It's almost like dating: they get wooed and they say, 'Oh, I've found the one.' And you meet the person and you say to yourself, *What were you thinking?*

"Leaders do this all the time. Sometimes leaders will bring people into their organizations, not out of wisdom, but to satisfy their own state of need. They have gotten into situations where they're overwhelmed and there's some aspect of leadership, of the team, of the organization, or of the business that they don't possess the skills for and then somebody shows up with that strength. All of a sudden here's their rescuer. But they didn't do their due diligence and a complete diagnosis. They might have gotten a strong person in that area of need, but they also got a kook in fourteen other areas. So you wind up going to lawyers and paying big money to get out of that hole."

The lightness of the moment had quickly changed to somberness as everyone in the circle recognized the validity of Henry's diagnosis. I suspect that each of us standing there could identify one, if not several, instances in which we had been guilty of exactly the foolishness Henry was describing. I remembered reading about this in his book *Integrity*, and thought about the wake-up call these insights had been to me. After all, how many nightmares had each of us hired, hoping for salvation, only to wind up in a mess of our own making?

"One of the problems is when leaders don't know their own impulses, blind spots, and weaknesses. I like it when I hear a leader say, 'Okay, we've got to hire a new person, and I have a tendency to have a blind spot with A, B, or C, so I want you guys to be in the interview process with me.' And then they set up systems to enable that to happen.

"An important phrase to me in leadership development is *ready, aim, fire*," Henry described, providing a more comprehensive perspective on the hiring process. "You have some leaders who are 'fire, ready, aim,' and they do things impulsively. You have others who are 'ready, ready, ready, ready, ready, ready,' and they can't ever pull the trigger. Wise leaders have systems and people in place with a timeline, and they don't allow themselves to hire someone by skipping or going around the process. You've got to make sure that you know your blind spots and that there are systems, processes, and people involved in doing the due diligence. Sometimes it all has to be done fast, but it doesn't mean there can't be a process to it."

Sam Chand had been listening intensely to the exchange. He brought up another helpful point, adding a new twist to the hiring process.

"When I was a university president I sometimes hired people for whom there was no job, and I created a job for them. I knew they would add value. In most situations I had a job vacancy with a job description and filled it, but once in a while I would run across marvelous, gifted individuals who were available for a short period of time and I had an opportunity to reel them in."

That outside-the-box thinking resonated with Rich Stearns. He introduced the aspect of seeking to align people with their strengths.

"For the most part you try to find people with the right skill sets to do a particular job. However, I think a shrewd leader also looks at people who are already in the organization." He paused for a second and then offered an example. "One of our major-donor fund-raisers is a woman who is a very gifted speaker, who tells stories about World Vision. So rather than pigeonhole her and say, 'Your job is not to do public speaking; it is to raise money from major donors,' we said, 'You know what? We're going to change the shape of the hole that your peg fits in, because you've got some unique qualities that we would be foolish not to take advantage of.' So this woman probably speaks about twenty times a year for World Vision to women's groups in particular, but sometimes to other donor groups. She adds a lot of value by doing that while using her giftedness and still serving as a fund-raiser for World Vision. And she may not raise as much money in her fund-raising job as some of the other reps

> *Wise leaders have systems and people in place with a timeline, and they don't allow themselves to hire someone by skipping or going around the process.*

that we have, but it's an accommodation to recognize that we need to make room in this organization for someone like this."

Rich has orchestrated several major reorganizations of World Vision during his tenure, responding to both changes in the marketplace and shifts in his workforce. I asked him how those adventures in restructuring related to his thinking.

"When I reorganize our team, I look at how to best reorganize around the gifts of my players. It's kind of like being a football coach, where at some point you look at the players you've got and ask what's the best way to utilize them. Your marketing VP might have certain skill sets that are unique and that you had built around, but when he leaves, you've got to realize that the next person might not have the same skill sets, and you might want to shift some of those responsibilities to maximize what you can do with your team."

It seemed like the right time to turn the corner and dive into the nasty part of human resources: addressing people's performance. Knowing that this was one of my own areas of weakness, I didn't want to bias the discussion by focusing on my personal deficiencies, so I led the conversation into the arena of setting expectations. We'd get to dealing with the failure to meet the expectations soon enough.

"Well, there's going to have to be some discipline," admitted Colleen, who had been listening carefully since starting us off on this line of exploration. She gave us a peek at how personnel matters are handled at Southwest. "We are not going to have a lot of rules, but the rules and the expectations we have for our employees are very, very important. And just like parenting, as long as you outline what the expectations are, then you can hold them accountable. You can't do that if you don't tell them the boundaries and standards, and you can't be disciplined if you don't discipline yourself and if you are not accountable."

She placed the role of expectations in context for us. "You have to remember, we have a real passion to serve our customers, but we are also very employee focused. So our pyramid is employees first, passengers second, shareholders third. Now I am not telling you that you will have a comedian every time you get on our airline or that somebody is going to sing, but I am telling you that you will find warm people. Generally speaking, you can tell they like what they do. My goal is that the person you see loading your bag or serving you a drink or checking you in demonstrates the same personality, attitude, demeanor, and behavior that you would see from that person if you happened to be his or her next-door neighbor. I don't want one personality at home and one at work."

Colleen touched on something I had discovered in our own research among effective parents: the importance of setting expectations, holding children accountable, and being consistent in upholding the standards and modeling them. Clarity and consistency. It struck me that she had even alluded to parenting in describing effective personnel leadership. My reflection on the parallels was broken by Jimmy Blanchard's contribution.

"We want to retain the very best people we have. We want the people who are average and mediocre to be the ones to leave, not the very best. And so we try to have a fast enough track to keep the very best people satisfied, happy, challenged, and motivated—feeling appreciated and invested in. What we find is the ones who can't keep up feel the pressure, and a lot of them will migrate out voluntarily."

But what about people who reach a level at which they prove to be incompetent or inefficient? What about employees who develop a lousy attitude? What do you do with people who cease to grow, or who lose their passion for the vision? How do you handle someone who is a poor teammate?

A smiling Sam Chand was the first to volunteer his thoughts on the subject. "I ask myself one simple question, George: is this person a *can't* or a *won't*? Can't is about abilities. We can help these kinds of people in most cases—not in all cases, but in most. But won't is about attitude. If the issue is attitude, the time to let that person know there is a problem is now, because here is the deal: we hire people for what they know and fire them for who they are. I'll hire Bill because he can do wonders with computers, but I'll fire him because he won't get along with anybody. If the issue is that he can't figure out how to do something, I can work with that. I will put together a plan that is manageable and measurable. He knows he must meet certain benchmarks. But if it's an attitude issue, like he doesn't get along with people, then he is cancer. When you remove cancer you are better off."

Sam's statement—you hire for what they know and fire for who they are—struck me like a baseball bat. If nothing else, it reasserted the significance of a person's character, and the importance that John had attached to evaluating character up front. I knew that Rich had spent a lot of time and energy dealing with these very issues at World Vision and was pleased that he reentered the conversation, following up on Sam's input.

"All of us have flat sides and strong sides in our personalities, our management styles, our skill sets. And one way to look at a person in your organization is in terms of his or her assets and liabilities. You want people who have a long list of assets and a short list of liabilities. In other words, the cost to enjoy the assets or skills they bring to the table—in terms of their liabilities—is minor. We all have liabilities. We all have things that we don't do well or problems that we sometimes can cause in an organization. So what you look for is a nice ratio between assets and liabilities.

"Where it gets dicey is when you get people who have a long list of assets but also a long list of liabilities. They add tremendous value because of their giftedness and their creativity and their ideas, but you pay a pretty steep price to get all of that from them because they might be abusive to people, or terrible collaborators, and they create tension in the organization.

"One of the things that is crucial is attitude. If you've got someone who has an attitude of 'I want to improve; I realize I have weaknesses and shortcomings and I'm willing to work hard to address them,' that means a lot. Somebody who says, 'Look, I don't think I need to change. It's not my problem; it's Fred's problem or it's Mary's problem'—somebody who's never willing to own up to his or her own part of the issue—it's hard to fix an attitude like that. It's hard to work with somebody who has the attitude that he or she is right and everybody else is wrong. So for me, if somebody doesn't have the attitude of self-improvement or self-criticism, I can't really work with that person."

Everyone in the group seemed to have experienced such people. But what's the solution?

"At that point, I've probably got to move the person out because I need somebody who's got a better attitude than that," Rich stated matter-of-factly. "I tend to believe that you can't fix every problem in a person. You can't change the leopard's spots. You can make the spots a little brighter or a little dimmer, but you can't necessarily change the spots—and that presumes he or she would be willing to go through it to begin with. Sometimes you've got people who are just a square peg in a round hole. They don't have the skill sets to really succeed in the job. I've come to believe that we do them no favor by keeping them in a job that they're failing at."

Hire for what they know and fire for who they are.

Then Rich touched on the sensitive area. "The person who's a square peg is always going to fail in the round hole, but maybe there's a square hole for that peg, a place where that person really can fit in, a job he or she can succeed at. Sometimes that job is in your organization, but sometimes it will be in another organization. So you have to see if there's a place within your organization where that person can actually add value, and if there's not, for whatever reason, then it's best for all parties if the person leaves."

I noticed through the body language, as well as the words and demeanor of these high-caliber leaders, that nobody enjoys firing coworkers. These were not the "I'll eat you for lunch" kind of leaders who needed to impose their authority at the expense of others in their path. But it was just as obvious that great leaders have the backbone to make the tough calls and to do so in a way that respects those whom they fire.

Rich continued with a war story about firing a high-profile executive. "You know, I once fired a guy at Lenox who was a VP and was failing. The day I fired him I said to him, 'I hate to do this, Bob. I can tell you it hurts me more than it hurts you. You won't believe me, but I take no joy in this. But I believe that a year from today we'll be able to talk about this and you'll be able to say, "Rich, leaving my job at Lenox turned out to be a really good thing."' I said, 'I think you're a very gifted person. You've got a lot of talents and a lot to offer. And when you find the right place to offer that, you're going to feel great. But you'd probably never leave Lenox on your own steam and so I'm the one who has to do it.' He said, 'I doubt it, Rich. I've worked at Lenox ten years, and this is pretty much the worst day of my life to hear that you're letting me go.' A year later he called me. He was at another company. I asked how he was doing and he said, 'I love what I'm doing. People love me here. I love the culture of this organization. You were right. I'm in a much better place today than I was a year ago.' So I kind of did him a favor. It was hard for me, and he didn't buy it at the time, but it turned out to be a favor."

Listening to that story made me appreciate the way that Rich had handled the experience: he was gentle but honest with his colleague. That tone resonated with Jimmy Blanchard, too, and he added a story of his own.

"When we have problems with someone, we don't decide it is not going to work at the first instance of trouble. We have frank conversations. We reiterate our values and say, 'This is who we are, this is the way we do it, and apparently you have some problem with that.' And if a person really has a problem with it, he or she will usually say so, and we will usually say pretty quickly that it's going to be better for him or her and for us if we part ways and he or she goes somewhere else and does something else. But it's important to us to treat folks right—with respect, admiration, consideration, and appreciation. If we find a leader in our organization who is mean spirited or manipulative—you know, he says the right thing to the boss but then beats up on people—we won't allow that.

"Everybody who works for us has a right to work for a good boss. A good boss is one who is edifying, who is interested in your future and your growth and your career, and whom you admire and respect and appreciate because he admires and respects and appreciates you. So if we find a leader who is not that kind of person, we have that conversation to tell him that it is not going to work here and he doesn't have a future here. To drive that home, I told all of our employees, 'I'm going to guarantee you that you are not going to have to work for that kind of supervisor. And if this organization doesn't fulfill that commitment to you—if you have a boss who is mean spirited or manipulative or who jerks you around, a command-and-control type, and we don't do something about it, you've got no reason to ever believe anything I tell you again."

How gutsy is that? I asked Jimmy if that cemented people's loyalty to the company and raised the commitment to excellence. He grimaced and noted a different outcome before such a positive outcome was realized.

"Well, first off we had probably 150 departures. In some cases, they were really good people, real contributors. But they were not respectful of other people and their work, and they were right to go. It was hard, but in the end we were a lot better off, and it helped to create an environment of trust. And the next time I stood up and said, 'We are going to do X, Y, and Z,' everybody was thinking, *I bet they are going to do it.*"

Rich picked up where Jimmy left off. "Sometimes if people don't really share the mission, vision, and values of the organization, they probably ultimately do need to move on. When I arrived at World Vision ten years ago I became a proponent of greater fiscal responsibility and the greater use of standard business practices to create efficiencies. What happened was kind of miraculous. People often said to me, 'You must have come in and fired a bunch of people, cleaned house.' Actually, in my first two years I don't think I fired one person or one vice president. A number of them read the writing on the wall and left. I think they recognized that they would not fit very well in the new paradigm, so they found other jobs. If a leader can cast the right vision and get the organization to buy into it, people who are uncomfortable with that often figure that out by themselves and find another place to serve.

"But occasionally there are people who don't see that, and they stay and they become a burr in the saddle. In those cases you try to win them over and persuade them to join the great cause or to sign up for the direction that the senior leadership is trying to go. But ultimately, if they refuse to do so and are recalcitrant, then you have to make a decision for them."

Henry had listened with interest to the most recent comments. His broad experience with leaders in many settings, plus his clinical psychology training and practice, had provided him with a deep understanding of the hiring-firing process.

"Firing is not done well often enough because when firing is done well, it's almost a nonevent. And here's why: If you've got someone who's not performing or someone who's performing but is a problem for other reasons, a good leader is involved in a process.

"A good leader, among other things, is an immune system for the organization. The leader has to guard the mission, guard the culture, guard the organization. So if you've got somebody who's not performing under your leadership, first of all you wouldn't want that lack of performance or that problem to continue and grow and spread. Good leadership means you've already entered into that problem with that person way back, before you get to firing. You would already have sat down and said, 'You know, this is an issue and I want this to work, and I want us to reach our goals. We've talked about what you need to do, but right now, you're not there. I want you to get there. Let's talk about how you can get there and how I can help you.'

"And the 'there' comes and things have not turned out as expected. Now we have a different kind of conversation, one that's no longer just about performance. The next conversation is, 'We've talked about this and we've given it time, we've given it resources, and we still have the problem. So now we've got a different kind of problem. Why hasn't that worked?'

"So you address this situation. You're upping the amperage on this to where the person knows that he or she is in a process that's going to result either in reaching the bar or leaving the company. By the time it happens, it's clear. We've set a time for it. If X happens, you're here. If Y happens, you're not there. And on the last day you sit there and say to them, 'We both know why we're sitting here.' And they say, 'Yeah, we know why we're here.' That's how it works when it's done well."

Henry's words rekindled in me the realization that good leadership is so often about applied common sense. All he had described, really, was setting standards and communicating regularly with people about whether or not they are meeting the agreed-upon standards. But the other thing that came to mind was one of my favorite quotes, from Mark Twain: "Common sense ain't." So I asked Henry, "Since the process is so simple, why don't leaders use it more often?"

"Here's the problem," he said, anticipating that one of us would ask that question. "It takes an integrated character to do this. If leaders have difficulty with hurting people's feelings—if they don't know the difference between hurt and harm, realizing that sometimes we have to hurt each other—they won't go there. The Bible says the wounds of a friend are better than the kisses of an enemy. You know that when a surgeon operates on you it's hurtful, but it doesn't harm you. So leaders have to learn to inflict hurt instead of harm. What I mean by that is that if they can learn to discipline and train people well, then they can do this well. If they can't—if they shy away from it, they avoid it, they wait too long until the cancer has spread—then they've often got a legal problem when they try to get rid of someone, because they don't have a paper trail or a process that makes the firing fair or just. At that stage it's just a mess.

"So you get back to character and the ability to have the conversation. You get into the way the organization is designed so that those cancers can't grow. An important part of this is giving managers and leaders good training in how to have these conversations and how to have the kind of relational leadership where these problems emerge around the table long before a bad firing has to take place." Henry then alluded to comments that Lou and Ralph had made earlier. "A lot of people get attached to people, and because of the friendships they can't pull the trigger and fire them. They forget they're stewards over the organization and that its mission and the number one rule, when it comes to leadership, is never hire anybody you can't fire. That's like getting in a car and giving the steering wheel to somebody else. If you're the leader, ultimately you've got to be able to demand a certain standard and expectations and have the ability to enforce that."

It was getting close to the time for me to run on stage again and transition into the next session. Before I made my exit, John Townsend affirmed Henry's words and piggybacked onto them.

"A good leader needs to know how to fire people. And I think the best advice that I give people is that it's got to be direct. A lot of times people don't want to hear 'No,' and when someone tells them 'No' they hear 'Maybe.' So if you're not very clear with the no, you can really cause lots of heartache and problems, even liability lawsuits over time. So be clear about it.

"At the same time be specific," John added. "And not only specific, but make sure you document it, that you have a paper trail, so that if anything happens, either on an emotional level or on a legal level, you can say, 'Here was our due diligence. We tried to cure this with the person. We took these steps, we did these HR things.' That way it becomes clear that you didn't just react, but that you really went the second and third mile to keep that person and cure the issue. Then you know you can sleep at night because it was a good way to fire the person and it was done well."

Somehow, firing a person and sleeping well at night were not activities that I would normally have put in the same sentence. But having heard the wisdom of these leaders, it all made sense. Leadership is, in many ways, applied common sense—even when it comes to hiring, nurturing, and firing people.

CHAPTER 7

LEADING
WELL

HAVE YOU EVER BEEN in the midst of a hurricane? That's what the morning at the Master Leader Conference felt like to me. My rushing back and forth between onstage duties and the engaging conversations in the greenroom had my head spinning. But I could not imagine being in a better place on earth. The ideas being bantered back and forth were tremendous. If I did not emerge a better leader after this experience, there probably wasn't much hope for me.

You know how sometimes your mind seems to latch onto a random thought that is tangentially related to your experience in that moment? I suddenly had one of those experiences as the series of commercials run by a credit card company took center stage in my brain.

Airfare: $459. Hotel: $159. Breakfast in the coffee shop: $12. Time spent with thirty of the nation's top leaders: priceless.

As I reached the greenroom again, having just sent the crowd off for lunch, I took a deep breath and made a beeline for the adjoining room, which had been set up for lunch among my colleagues. The last thing I wanted to do was miss out on more of the exchanges taking place among these men and women.

Upon reaching the large, well-appointed room, I got everyone's attention, asked Chaplain Black to say the blessing for us before the food arrived, and then instructed everyone on the lunch protocol and our schedule. Before everyone sat around the table, I again thanked them for their presence, indicated how successful the morning had been, and expressed my excitement about the interaction taking place backstage. Then I seized the moment to launch our focus at lunchtime.

"As the servers bring in our food, I am going to throw out a question for us to discuss. All of you have incredible track records of leading well. If someone were to ask you, point-blank, what it takes to lead well, how would you answer such a question?"

There was the usual good-natured griping about such a broad question, but I could already see some of the members of our group reflecting on how to answer the inquiry. As the doors swung open and the catering staff carried in the trays with food, I tried to restore our focus, asking, "Who wants to break the ice for us?"

With a room full of leaders, bashful behavior was not likely to be an issue. Sure enough, several people showed an inclination to get the ball rolling, and I nodded at Rich Stearns to open our conversation.

"Perhaps the two most important jobs of a leader that I would have are, number one, setting and casting a vision that sets the sights of the people in the organization on a tangible goal that is palpable, energizing, and exciting. Number two, after casting the vision, the most powerful leverage a leader has is in the selection of the people who will carry out the vision. Finding the right people with the right skills and putting them in the right jobs and then turning them loose ends up being incredibly powerful. This is no new revelation for leaders or management, I realize, but I really do think these are important."

We were off to a good start. "Great thoughts, Rich, thanks for getting us off the ground. Let me dissect that bit," I said. "Rich's ideas could be separated into two larger streams of dialogue—the role of people in leading well, and the role of action that stems from the identification and casting of vision. And based on some of the morning's conversations in the green-room, we might even think about a third aspect of what it takes to lead well, and that's the mentality of a leader. If we look at those three dimensions, what would you counsel someone about how to lead well?"

The vision theme drew Lou Holtz into the conversation. "My philosophy of leadership is simply this: You need a vision for where you want the organization to go. The second thing you need is a concrete plan that's going to enable you to be successful. Point number three is that you have to lead by example. You cannot talk about greatness if you don't pursue it yourself, and you can't talk about working hard if you don't work hard. Number four, as a leader, you've got to hold people accountable. Too many people in a leadership role worry about being popular or well liked. Your obligation is to make people the very best they could possibly be, and the only way that can be done is to get them out of their comfort zones and to believe in them more than they believe in themselves. Anytime you push an individual toward greatness, it's because you believe he or she is capable of greatness. And when you hold him or her accountable and you have standards, you can't have those standards so that you'll look good. Point number five is you cannot compromise your core values. Core values are what hold the country together. They hold a business together. They hold a family together. They hold a team together. You don't have to like the same music, clothing, food—you don't even have to like each other personally. But you all have to share the same core values. You cannot compromise on those. Everybody in the organization must understand your core values. In every place I've been the coach, the core values were simple: we're going to trust each other, we're committed to excellence, and we're going to care about each other. I won't compromise on those."

As I watched Coach Holtz speak about his nonnegotiables, I was again struck by the fact that leaders are people of conviction. They include other people in the activity they generate and direct, but once good leaders latch onto elements that they deem to be critical to the success of their leadership, you cannot jar them loose from those things. Looking at the passion Coach has for his core values, it was unthinkable that you could possibly get him to lighten up on trust, excellence, or caring. I'd heard him tell enough stories from his past that I understood how deeply held those values are in his heart. And I was beginning to see that quality in all of these great leaders.

Newt Gingrich had a big smile on his face as he listened to Coach Holtz. After complimenting the coach on his leadership and his insights into the process, the former Speaker of the House offered his own parallel assessment of what it takes to be an effective leader.

"To be a great leader you have to do three things that are very hard. First, you have to teach in a way that others can learn. One of my ground rules is that all communication occurs in the mind of the listener or the reader. Second, you have to be able to articulate vividly with emotional and moral power what you are rallying people to do. And finally, you have to live it. You have to personify it. If you do those things, then you're in a different league. Ronald Reagan was almost always the same person—the same genial, self-comforting style. You could take comfort in the certainty of who Reagan was at all times. In order for leaders to be followed they have to have such consistency that it has to be like putting on a mask, because no one could ever internally live with that level of consistency."

That stirred up the group, and the room became a beehive of animated discussion in clusters, dissecting and expanding on the ideas already put on the table. After a minute or two I tried to redirect our focus. Newt had been asked for some clarification by several people, so he responded to some of those requests.

"Leadership is about listening, learning, helping, and leading—in that order. I had to learn to listen, because I would never have been allowed to lead the people of Georgia if I'd remained a transient army brat with no connections. Listening is trying to understand what people are saying and what it means to them. It's called appreciative understanding: you try to understand literally what they're saying and why it makes sense to them. That doesn't mean you have to agree or sympathize, but it does mean you're learning all day. Your life becomes a permanent university."

As people thanked Newt for his clarification, Coach Holtz indicated that he wanted to add one more thought to his prior contribution too. Having heard what was being said, he recognized that one of his natural tactics had been omitted from what he had said earlier.

"Maybe the most important thing is you must explain to everybody in the organization how they're going to benefit when you reach the goal. If you have not helped everybody in the organization to understand how it's in their best interest to reach the goal, then they aren't going to buy into it and they'll be a negative influence on other people when they're away from you."

That seemed like a good segue to getting some input regarding the importance of people in the leadership endeavor, so I asked if the group had some ideas regarding how people fit into what it takes to lead well.

Rich Stearns set the tone for this portion of our dialogue. "Finding the right people with the right skills and putting them in the right jobs is important. Young leaders," he explained, by which he meant those who have not had much experience, "often make the mistake of thinking, 'I got here because I'm smart and I'm capable, and since there's nobody more capable than I am I'll just do all this work myself.' What that results in is micromanaging. Making the transition to leadership means a young leader has to go from being a doer to a coach."

With a respectful nod to Coach Holtz, Rich continued. "A good coach understands that he's got to create the environment within which the players can be successful, but he's got to let the players do their thing. The coach leads from the sidelines and in between the games so that when the players get on the field they're productive and get the good results. You have to avoid the temptation to intervene and do things for the people whom you've selected, but instead recognize that they're the ones who have the right gifts to do what has to be done. You become a generalist instead of a specialist, more like the conductor of the orchestra than the first violinist, trying to get the most out of all the players."

The coaching metaphor had clearly struck a chord with our group. It was continued by General Dees. "John Wooden, in his great book *They Call Me Coach*, wrote, 'Life is a united effort of many.' He described his success as a coach at UCLA as an outgrowth of understanding unity and team building. The coach needs to be part of the team, not external to the team. You cannot have a united effort of many unless you are part of the team."

From my own experiences with leaders around the world I know how hard that is to facilitate. Leaders often feel isolated or separated from their group. It takes intentional effort to feel like an equal within the group. Some were expressing variations on that theme when I overheard Colleen Barrett speaking with the people sitting next to her.

"Part of leadership is knowing when to follow. You have to know when to get out of the way." What a great insight! Leading is not always about being in front; sometimes a leader must allow others whom he or she has empowered to take the reins for a while. Great leaders sometimes put themselves out of a job by raising up other leaders who are competent and ready to provide direction.

So we had established the importance of selecting the right people to lead, building unity among them, removing one's ego from the process, and confidently turning people loose so they can do what they do best. Were there other significant dimensions to the people aspect of leading well? Thankfully Warren Bennis spoke up, addressing the need for a sense of collaboration.

"People like vulnerability. And it's appropriate in a leader. You see, it's all about relationships. Leading is about having a goal to achieve with a group of people—let's call them your followers or your associates. Leadership is when the leader works within the great collaboration of his or her followers to achieve a great goal."

"But why, then, aren't more people great leaders?" I asked. "If working together is a hallmark of great leaders, what holds leaders back from that?"

Again, a number of smaller conversations immediately sprang forth, and from what I could tell, the gist was that it often seems that many leaders are more interested in establishing themselves as being superior to or better than the people they lead—smarter, more willing to take risks, more experienced, better communicators, or whatever. One particular comment in the mix stood out to me. John Ashcroft nonchalantly stated, "Everybody has great worth. People who believe that everybody has great worth are likely to be great leaders." That seemed to me like a foundational perspective that every leader needs to possess. You cannot give people the dignity they deserve unless you believe they have worth; and people will not follow you unless you give them the dignity they need.

I heard a portion of what Henry Cloud was saying to those around him, and he, too, was onto something important. "The ability to not only build but to maintain trust is necessary. Ultimately a leader has got to get done whatever he or she is getting done through and with and by people. As Stephen Covey has said, when trust breaks down, speed decreases and costs increase. When trust is high, speed is high, so we can get things done faster and the costs are lower. The whole trust dimension is huge."

I made a note to focus on "the whole trust dimension" during one of our greenroom sessions; it felt too critical to shortchange in the limited time we had left during our lunch break. But it also seemed as if we were ready to touch on the mind of the leader. In fact, after taking a sip of water and listening to some of the feedback that his prior comment raised, Henry continued to discuss what it takes to lead well, emphasizing aspects of the leader's mentality.

"Good leaders have the ability to be oriented toward truth and reality. A lot of people have biases and blind spots. They have blinders on; they have past experiences that color their vision of how they see people or how they see realities. But then there are other people who have a real orientation toward being able to see reality and aren't afraid to call things like they are. They are able to confront the brutal realities and, at the same time, maintain hope. So leadership is more than honesty. It's having a hunger, not only to tell the truth, but to be finding truth and reality. The best leaders are the ones who have a voracious appetite for finding out what that reality is."

Years ago I had read that one leadership training group had described leadership as making sense of reality for people, and helping them to shape that reality. Listening to Henry's words, it sounded like discovering and redefining reality would take considerable measures of courage, self-confidence, and a willingness to make mistakes. Newt tacked on his thoughts to that sentiment.

"You have to surround yourself with people who can fire you. And you need to be in the company of people who don't mind saying that you're wrong." Instantly I thought there was probably no place on earth where you were more likely to be surrounded by people who do not hesitate to tell you when you are wrong than the U.S. Congress! But Newt's points were germane and well-taken—and they sparked some reaction from Bob Dees, who recalled some recent army history.

"In the 1970s the army was broken due to drugs, Vietnam, and all the other cultural experiences going on at the time. In the 1980s there was a training revolution in the army that was technologically driven, through the adoption of MILES—which stands for Multiple Integrated Laser Engagement System. It allowed you to go from a subjective to an objective assessment of your training reality. That started an amazing chain of events, which allowed for questions that evaluated causality and prevention or improvement. It created a whole learning culture in the U.S. Army.

"You have to recognize reality before you can continue to grow," Bob summarized. "A wise senior executive is well served if he can scan his domain and identify his teachable moments. You can coach or teach all day long, but if it's not done during those teachable moments, when the people are ready to learn, what difference does it make if you've been teaching? A wise leader perceives those teachable moments and then provides his coaching. A leader has to be constantly alert for those moments."

Clearly, then, educating people about reality is an important aspect of a leader's job. But Professor John Kotter added another level of intrigue to this dimension of leading well, arguing for the development of a sense of urgency in discerning and reshaping that reality.

"In an increasingly fast-moving and volatile world, organizations have got to get better at changing or morphing to the next stage in their development. But the first step is about creating a sufficient sense of urgency. This sense of urgency is becoming more important, because it keeps people hyperalert to all of the things that are going on out there that are either opportunities or hazards and will require some adjustments and flexibility and changes inside. When they've got that sense, people are just so much more determined to not only look every day at what's going on, but to act on what they see and to do something about it. They are more likely to get up every single day determined to act on the big opportunities or hazards— and that's a huge asset in a world that's not standing still, particularly when the average organization doesn't have that same sense of urgency at all."

After some more discussion on this matter, I turned to Henry and asked if there were any other elements he felt were indispensable to leading effectively. He had more to offer.

"Good leaders have an orientation toward results. There's a big difference between leaders and those who are just theorizers, or contemplators, or armchair quarterbacks. People who really lead just cannot exist in a world that does not create very tangible results. They are very results oriented. I think that the best leaders are the ones who lean toward creating tangible results as opposed to getting in the way of those results."

Nobody seemed inclined to disagree with this point. Leaders generate results. That was kind of a no-brainer. But, to me, the question was *how* they get significant results. My guess is that bad leaders are interested in generating positive results but don't know how. What distinguishes the two groups?

"Good leaders have a very broad view of everything. If they're at the top of the organization, they really do have a 360-degree sense, internally and externally," explained John Kotter. "That's just the way good leaders are. But another part of the breadth is that they not only see, but also feel some responsibility for that breadth. Great leaders, because they're so broad in their thinking, think about the scope of their responsibility. In business, the notion that 'My job is to maximize shareholder wealth' would never occur to a good leader, you know? Certainly my job is to make sure that the people who give us financing get a really, really good deal. But my job is also to make sure that the people who buy our products and services get good products and services at good prices. And my job is to make sure that our employees have good jobs and good careers. And my job is also to make sure that we don't pollute the communities we operate in, and so forth. That's just what good leaders think."

There were sighs of acknowledgment around the room as these leaders accepted John's description of the weight of responsibility that good leaders embrace. The reaction was not a feeling of heaviness about that responsibility as much as it was about having a commitment, as Coach Holtz had put it, to "do what's right." And such a responsibility has a measure of breadth that the average person would neither comprehend nor handle with poise.

As a break in the conversation occurred, I turned back to Henry and raised my eyebrows, wondering if he had more components to add to his list about what it takes to lead well. He did.

"Another item, I think, is that good leaders have an ability to embrace negative reality in a spirit of both grace and truth, as the Bible says. Psychologists refer to this as having a neutralized tone. In other words, when they get the bad numbers, they don't freak out; they embrace them. They see negative realities as just part of what leadership is. They get up in the morning and they go solve problems. They face the conflicts. They face the negative realities. They're not problem avoidant. And they do all of this without anger or fear. They've normalized it. They know that if they're facing problems they still have a pulse."

Good leaders have a very broad view of everything.

People laughed at Henry's description of good leaders—because they all knew what he had said was true, and that most people wanted nothing to do with the kind of headaches that leaders treat as just another day at the office. I asked Henry if the converse was also true: that if the leader was not facing problems, he or she would start to get a little bit worried and wonder what was going on.

"Yeah, exactly," he replied. "Good leaders are almost always on an active search to identify what needs to get better. It doesn't need to be something toxic that needs their attention, but they're always asking for the report because they want to know what's going on. They don't stick their heads in the sand."

Someone wisecracked that this mentality could easily become a leader's worst nightmare, as he digs up problems that were not evident and could perhaps have remained hidden from public view. Henry agreed that many people in leadership positions are fearful of uncovering the extent of what requires their leadership. "You see a lot of leaders who, when they get feedback or anything negative, will immediately say, 'Well, I don't need that negativity around here. What are all these naysayers doing here?' But that's just not the way the good ones are. The good ones don't even see a problem as a problem. They see it as part of leading.

"I was consulting in a situation yesterday where the organization was facing the threat of a lawsuit. Immediately the board and the leader of that division reacted defensively; they shut down the operation, and said, 'There's too much exposure here.' They got out of a real key area they needed to be in—and they did it out of fear. I knew that business pretty well and I was thinking, *There's no seasoned leadership in this room.* Seasoned leadership would have taken that letter, sat down, reviewed the merits, and figured out where their exposure was or if it was a frivolous, crazy suit. A seasoned leader would never allow a threat or a problem to dictate the mission statement, if you will. When negative news comes, good leaders have a certain kind of healthy detachment to be able to observe it, and it doesn't get all the stress hormones firing in their brains, which causes judgment to go out the window."

Many in the room had experienced similar instances where immature leadership had produced a train wreck for various organizations. Feeling affirmed, Henry moved forward with the next aspect of effective leadership.

"The fifth characteristic of those who lead well is they have an orientation toward increase. Leaders make things grow. They're not maintainers. To do that, they avoid gambling—but they also take risks. When you see good leaders taking risks it's really never a risk—it's a natural extension of the capacities that they've already built; they're just taking the next step. People will watch them and then say, 'Gosh, she really did well, but she took a big risk.' What those people really mean is, 'Well, she left the security of her job and she launched out.' But it really wasn't risky because she had spent ten years developing the abilities to bring to fruition what she was going to do, and all the necessary capacities were there, so there wasn't anything more risky about it than when a snake sheds its skin; she's just kind of grown out of the old constraints. When somebody goes from playing college ball to the pros, is that a risk? Well, no, it's a natural extension of the capacities and abilities that that person has built. So good leaders have an orientation toward increase.

"And then the last one, and this is arguably the most important, is that a good leader's character gives him or her an orientation toward transcendence. In other words, good leaders realize it's not about them; it's about things larger than they are, things that transcend them. It's really about the values, the people they serve, the constituents, the employees, the stockholders, the mission, and God Himself. The leaders who are the problem ones are those who say, 'I'm not God,' but if you follow them around they act like they are." A burst of laughter ensued as Henry concluded to a roomful of appreciative looks and nodding heads.

Several leaders wanted to get on the transcendence bandwagon. Seth Godin was first among them. He noted that in his work he had discovered that great leaders "are able to see, able to notice, able to sense what people really want, what they're afraid of, and where they want to go."

He underscored the fact that good leaders empower people to pursue and achieve those things.

As our time drew to a close, Patrick Lencioni put a wonderful bookend on a challenging discussion about leading well. "To be a great leader, you have to master two things at the same time, and they do not easily coexist. One is you have to be humble, meaning that you know you are not better than the people you lead. You are not more important, not more worthy. The CEO who runs the company and the janitor there are equally important as human beings. But on the other side, you have to believe your actions and words are more important than those of other people because they are watching you and following you. When I think of leadership, I think of being a servant, for sure, but being a servant leader means taking a position out in front of people, without making yourself out to be more important than the people you're serving as a leader."

Leaders make things grow.

That seemed to be a fitting ending to a fruitful lunchtime give-and-take. Patrick's notion of the leader as servant was a helpful reminder that great leaders serve people by using their ability to orchestrate change in order to create a better future. But his words also highlighted the fact that leadership is a study in paradoxes. There was no doubt in my mind that the discussions to come in the afternoon and the next day would raise yet more of the paradoxes that challenge leaders and those who study leadership.

CHAPTER 8

EARNING AND MAINTAINING TRUST

DURING THE LUNCH HOUR, Henry had raised the issue of trust. Having recently spent time with various leaders in China, getting a firsthand glimpse at how the government's history of oppression and stealth attacks against cultural leaders had bred an atmosphere of fear and mistrust, I had a special interest in this topic. I admired leaders who felt compelled to do what was right in an uncertain and unsafe environment, knowing that they would likely suffer for their choices. Things in China seem to have been changing for the better in recent years, but the past always influences the future. Building and maintaining trust with people is crucial to creating the capacity for getting people to continually pursue a vision of a future that transcends the known.

So after I got the afternoon session on track I returned to the green-room, hoping to get some of our leaders to describe what they have learned about trust. As things turned out, it wasn't a hard task at all. A number of my colleagues had clearly put a lot of thought into the matter—and everyone present had experienced the ups and downs of establishing and maintaining trust.

As a group of us gathered around one of the big-screen monitors to watch the opening minutes of the new session, I sheepishly mentioned that I was hoping to follow up on some of the ideas that had been bandied about during lunch. Toward that end, I asked no one in particular how a leader gains people's trust. Seth Godin gave an immediate and straightforward answer: "You have to trust them."

I let that sit there for a bit without responding, and Ralph Winter added some bulk to Seth's simple, albeit insightful, reply.

"Trust is letting people have as much rope as they need to be sure they feel good and they can deliver the goods," was Ralph's perspective. He related his idea to what he does on a movie set. "On a production, the crew knows that delivering is the marker; they have got to be ready when the camera is starting, and if they are not, they cannot do that too many times before they are gone. So trust is about the clarity of expectations and delivering."

The tall, bearded producer paused, looking at his feet while deep in thought, then added another aspect. "But it's also built on follow-through, on standing up for those people in a meeting. For instance, I gain their trust if they have done their job, and then I stand up for those people. If they have done well, then I earn their trust by protecting them and by making sure they share some of the attention that our efforts produce."

The notion of building trust by following through was acknowledged when Henry Cloud took the same concept and shifted our vantage point on it.

"I was recently working in a company, doing extensive interviews with all of the direct reports of several leaders. One person was comparing the current CEO to their previous leader and said, 'You know what? This guy's tougher, but it's really good, because no matter what's going on, I know he wants me to succeed. He really desires my best.' And so this person is willing to follow that leader and to do the hard things—and even give up things—because he doesn't question whether or not that leader wants the best for him. Establishing that kind of support is a big part of maintaining trust.

"But another huge part of maintaining trust is making sure that you do what you say," continued the psychologist. "To become more trusted and better followed, some leaders need to close the say-do gap, not by doing more, but by saying less. Some people respond to every request by saying, 'Oh, yeah, I can do that, sure, no problem.' That is overpromising. They think they're going to have people like them and will win them over by overpromising. But over time, people just don't believe them anymore. Leaders have to be very careful about what they say they're going to do. Don't open your mouth if you're not really going to do what you say, because people are watching you, overtly and covertly."

> *Trust is letting people have as much rope as they need to be sure they feel good and they can deliver the goods.*

So developing trust is closely related to integrity. Henry's writing and training partner, John Townsend, chipped in to build on Henry's point.

"Trust is more likely to emerge if you are an integrated person. That means you walk the talk, and the values and mission that are stated explicitly in the organization are values that people see in you. Honesty, encouragement, customer service, efficiency, taking care of the bottom line, caring about people, producing quality—we look to see if the person adheres to those things on a day-to-day basis and lives in that way. If so, we feel like that person is the real thing, the real deal.

"But trust is also created when leaders are an open book, when either they make a mistake or there's bad news they have to deliver. They are the first ones in line to say, 'Hey, I did this; I messed up the projections' or 'I handled that contract wrong and we missed a negotiation, and I'm sorry about that; it's my fault and I want to take full responsibility and help in any way I can to undo that.'"

The notion of being open, available, and even vulnerable to those with whom you work was something that Patrick Lencioni wanted to address.

"If a leader is not vulnerable, you can't and shouldn't trust him or her. To be a great leader you have to be vulnerable, you have to let people know who you are. Most people do not want to take advantage of a leader who is vulnerable. It takes a risk and leap of faith for a leader to be vulnerable, but almost every great leader I've seen is the kind of person who is comfortable being on display before his or her people. If you can't humble yourself, you don't deserve to be trusted. That's a hard thing, especially because they tell us, 'Don't let them see you sweat.' Really, we should say, 'Hey, check this out, look at this,'" he said, pointing to the sweat on his own brow. "The worst thing you can do is pretend you aren't sweating. So, to be humble you have to be vulnerable, which means disclosing things about yourself, letting people relate to you as an equal, and knowing it is not jeopardizing but enhancing your ability to lead them.

"One of the exercises we take people through is to go around the table and talk about where we grew up, how many kids were in our families, and what was the most challenging thing about our childhoods. When you hear the leader say he grew up poor and then talk about what happened when people made fun of him, or what happened to his family after his dad died, suddenly that leader is just another kid like you, and now you know who he is as a person. You can now admire and trust him."

The growing group had now shifted their attention from the flat screen back to our discussion. Bob Dees, the retired army general, had been respectfully listening to his peers talk about a subject that is dear to every military leader. I could tell that the conversation had stirred something inside of him, and I asked if he had any thoughts on this matter.

Bob spent a moment outlining a pair of gut-wrenching situations during which he was the leader in charge, times when lives were lost and many more were in jeopardy. "Sometimes, when there are serious situations—death or trauma—the best thing to do is just to be there. In crisis situations, you have to know when to hold 'em and when to fold 'em. You have to be very simple, compassionate, and succinct. As I think back upon the traumas—helicopter crashes or a train plunging off the track into fifty feet of water and nine soldiers drowning, things like that—sometimes it's what you don't say that's important. Sometimes, it's just being there with your people that builds their trust in you."

His insight—that mere presence in the midst of people when they need to draw upon the strength that a leader possesses—was a powerful one. That strength, though, must come from people's sense that the leader is not just a victim standing by, but someone who has the ability to guide and direct people in any situation, no matter how good or bad. Tony Dungy put some flesh on those bones with his observations about the importance of being competent and lending that strength to those who need it.

"A leader gains trust by demonstrating proficiency. You have to earn that confidence from your group by demonstrating that you know where you are going and that you have the ability to get them there. If the leader has the integrity that wins people to him, and works at developing their trust and confidence, he's going to have a better time when things are tough. It's pretty easy to lead downhill. The real test is when you have to go uphill; that's when people have to really dig in to follow you. As a leader, you are there for the benefit of everyone else, trying to help them get to where they need to go and to be as good as they can be. And that's why they are following, because they believe that you can help them be better, that you can help them reach the goals they have."

Miles McPherson was on the same wavelength as his fellow football pro. Miles, who had retired from the NFL more than a decade ago, suggested that such proficiency is impossible unless the leader is consistent in what he or she provides to his or her people.

"People, by nature, want predictability. When people look at a leader, they want to know what they are going to get and when they are going to get it. If the leader delivers, that's consistency, and if you are consistent, people will respect you. You don't have to agree with them to get their respect and trust, but you have to be consistent. If you tell the truth all the time, they will respect you. That's consistency. If people know what they're going to get, they will feel they can trust that leader because he or she is predictable."

Coach Dungy nodded approvingly and added a few words about how consistency affects people's trust. "I have a lot of discussions with my team about all kinds of things, including how I'm going to make decisions and what those decisions will be based on," he explained. "In doing so, I'm trying to be a person whom they can trust. I want them to hear and see that my decisions don't change with circumstances. I am always going to do what I think is best for the team, and for the individuals on the team. I want the guys to know that."

We hadn't heard much from Wilson Goode, the former mayor of Philadelphia, during the day. He had been attentive, but Wilson is a quiet, dignified person who seems to feel no need to share his opinion simply because he has one. You cannot help but like him; he has a reserved but authoritative air about him. He looked as if he wanted to engage on this topic, so I invited him to share his thoughts about building trust.

A leader gains trust by demonstrating proficiency.

"First, you have to meet people where they are, and understand where they are and what they are going through, and know them as they are, not as someone else perceives them to be. People trusted me because they knew that I knew them, and I was there with them.

"But developing trust is also about forming relationships. Even before I became mayor, before I had any public office at all, I had developed relationships with people all across the city. Those relationships were based upon people knowing me and knowing my heart and not just what they had read about me. Part of transformation has to do with relationships; you cannot get to transformation without having relationships with God and with other people."

As we digested Wilson's words, I noticed that Ken Blanchard had snuck up behind the soft-spoken mayor to hear what he had to say. Wilson is one of Ken's friends. Okay, everybody who meets him becomes one of

Ken's friends! But Ken had listened with obvious delight to what Wilson expressed and then provided some of his own experiences and wisdom on the matter of building trust.

"I wrote a book with the two top whale trainers at Sea World because I was concerned about this trust issue. I had been asking people around the world, 'How do you know whether you're doing a good job?' The number one response was, 'Nobody's yelled at me lately.' Well, you cannot build trust when you're doing that. So at Sea World I asked a group of people, 'How many of you think that it would be a good idea to punish an eleven-hundred-pound killer whale and then tell the trainers to get in the water with it?' Of course they all laughed."

Ken is a wonderful storyteller. That's one of the skills that so many great leaders use to their advantage: disarming people through the method while engaging and educating them with the content. Ken went on to the point of his story. "It turns out there are key things the trainers do. The first thing is they build trust. When they get a new whale, whether it's a baby or one from another facility, they don't do any training for almost a month. All they do is feed it and play with it. I asked, 'Why do you take so long?' One trainer said, 'We want to convince the new whales we mean them no harm.' Trust is based on the belief that you do not mean them harm. That doesn't mean you're not going to give people feedback or hold them accountable.

"Trust is knowing that I'm not going to make some arbitrary, off-the-wall decision that impacts you without involving you in the process, because I'm your partner. I'm not your superior and you're not my subordinate. We just have different roles."

Talking about relationships, and their impact on developing trust, affirmed some of Jon Gordon's work. He explained what he had learned in that regard.

"As a leader, you can have the greatest vision in the world, but if you don't have relationships with the people you're leading, and those people don't trust you, they won't follow you. Coach Mike Smith [head coach, Atlanta Falcons football team] meets with every player on the team and establishes that relationship with them. He goes into the locker room to talk to them and even goes into the training room, where the players deal with injuries. That's highly unusual among coaches, but he does that because he has established that relationship with the players. They trust him because they know he cares about them."

One of my favorite people in the room was certainly Lou Holtz. Coach always has an amazing way of cutting to the heart of a matter and making it simple for others to understand. On various occasions I've heard him say that he is just a simple guy trying to make life simple for those who follow him. Perhaps it was Jon's narrative about a football coach building trust that brought Coach into the loop.

"If you do the right thing, you will have the trust of people. If you lie and cheat, if you're always on somebody's back, if you cheat on your wife, if you steal, you're not going have anybody's trust. And without trust, there can be no relationship. You can't be married if you can't trust each other. You can't have a football team if they can't trust each other."

Coach took a deep breath, looked a few people in the eye, and continued. "Now, I don't know of any other way that you can get people to trust you and to trust each other than to have everybody operate on the same rule, and that's *do what's right*. Let's look at Tylenol. Many years ago, Tylenol capsules were poisoned and some people died. What did Tylenol do? They took everything off the shelf and then came up with a tamper-proof bottle. Today, Tylenol is more successful than ever. Why did they do it? It was the right thing to do. Just doing the right thing is what builds trust. If you're going to lead, people have to trust you. And they've got to not only trust you; they've got to be able to trust each other. And I don't know of any other way you can trust each other than to get people to do the right thing. My wife and I have been married together ninety-four years—forty-seven apiece, but together that's ninety-four." People laughed as he brought it home. "How did we do that? We can trust one another. I never lose her trust. And the only way you can get that trust is by doing the right thing."

Glancing at the digital countdown clock next to the stage door, I realized that I had to head back onstage in a few minutes for the next changing of the guard. But before I left, I asked the assembled leaders if trust that is lost could ever be regained. How many leaders in business, government, and ministry have been front-page news in the past few years because they broke people's trust? Is it possible to restore trust once a leader has destroyed it? Mike Huckabee, perhaps sensing my need to rush off to handle my MC duties, made short work of the answer.

"It's possible, George, but it's twice as hard, and I'm not sure that it's ever given back at the same level as it was the first time. In the back of people's minds, they always wonder, *Will he do it to me again?*"

And with that realistic but sobering thought, I excused myself and headed for the stage. I could not afford to miss my cue to relieve the speakers currently on the platform. After all, I had just learned that part of being a good leader is developing trust with people, and a key route to establishing that trust is to do one's tasks with proficiency. The last thing I wanted to do was have my own need for learning how to lead get in the way of the needs of the people I was there to serve.

CHAPTER 9

CONFRONTATION AND CONFLICT

ON MY WAY TO THE STAGE, I was stopped by one of the stage managers, who instructed me on what to do during my next sequence. His idea seemed a bit crazy to me, and I felt uncomfortable following through on it. I told him about my discomfort and how the entire approach seemed inconsistent with the tenor we had built into the conference up to that point. He insisted that it be done his way. Noticing the director nearby, I waved him over and replayed what the stage manager had just told me to do and asked if that was indeed the way they wanted me to approach the coming segue. I again described my feeling that it did not seem like the best or even a logical way of building on what we had done up to that point.

Well, for an event that had run smooth as silk up to that point, we now had what certainly appeared to be a major behind-the-scenes flare-up in the making. I could feel the stage manager's eyes burning a hole in my face while I watched the director grow red with rage toward the stage manager.

He asked if I would excuse them for a moment, then pulled the stage manager ten feet farther into the bowels of the stage wing. A fierce argument ensued in subdued tones so as not to interrupt the proceedings on the main stage just thirty feet away. A few moments later, the stage manager stomped off in the opposite direction while the director took a second to compose himself and then rejoined me to say that I should continue with what we had originally planned for this segue.

A bit shaken by the confrontation, and having no idea what was behind it all, I nevertheless did my segment and then fled to the safety of the greenroom. But the experience still filled my mind. I figured, *What better way to get clarity on conflict and confrontation than to quiz the best leaders around about that whole can of worms?* My interest was not so much in the little episode I'd just experienced but in a broader understanding of how conflict and confrontation impact leadership.

After getting a cup of tea to calm my own nerves and taking a brief moment to collect my thoughts, I glanced around the room to see what was going on. I noticed that Henry Cloud was sitting on a couch, alone, watching Michael Franzese on one of the flat screens. I slowly moved toward Henry, knowing that he would have plenty of solid wisdom on the issue of conflict. I was aware that he had recently written *The One-Life Solution,* which had addressed confrontation in one section of the book.

After absorbing a few good-natured jabs over my incessant drilling for oil in this high-density field of knowledge and expertise, I explained my recent experience and the more general line of questioning about conflict and confrontation that it had stimulated. He rolled his eyes playfully, as if I was an incorrigible researcher—guilty as charged, I suppose—sat back in his chair, and began to impart the insights I was seeking.

His bemusement with me continued, even as he began his coaching session. "Two things are true about confrontation. One is that if it's difficult for you, don't worry; it can be learned and you can get better at it. The other is that if it's easy for you, then that could be a problem because it probably means you love to go beat up on people." We chuckled at this before he turned more serious.

"Naturally speaking, you can usually categorize people into one of three styles in terms of conflict. The first is people who are very aggressive about it, as if they're looking for a fight and they're going to win. We call them attorneys. That's their orientation: they are aggressive, they have a 'take no prisoners' attitude, and that's natural to them." Based on some experiences I'd had, I wasn't sure if he was joking or being serious. I came to see he was serious.

"The second is what we would call the 'moving away' style, where they want to avoid conflict. They don't like conflict and shy away from it. They try to go around it or not deal with it or somehow skirt it. Sometimes they'll send the hatchet man in to do it for them, but however it unfolds, they don't really want to be involved in it.

"The third style is what has been called a 'moving toward' approach, which involves being a peacekeeper rather than a peacemaker. They'll join the person and love him or her and smooth things over.

"Each of those styles is incomplete because it's not integrated. Leaders in conflict bring to the table all of their incompleteness, which is the biblical word for immaturity. When we have a conflict, if we haven't become mature or complete, we bring our needs to the table. Think of it this way. If you are a mechanic and you have a complete toolbox, then you go in, you diagnose the problem, and you use the tool that's needed, right? So in conflict, sometimes you confront, sometimes you listen, sometimes you understand, sometimes you agree to disagree. Sometimes, to your own surprise, you agree and you change to embrace the other side. Sometimes you have a dialogue in which a new answer emerges that transcends either position. But to do these you need a lot of skills, right?"

Henry's words had me thinking about my own responses to conflict. I've written some tough truths that people have disliked, resulting in all manner of conflict. I could associate the different tools he was describing with various instances of conflict I had faced in the past few years.

"George, you know the old saying that if all I have is a hammer, everything looks like a nail?"

"That's actually one of my favorite sayings," I told him. "I use it a lot when I'm coaching people, because there's a tendency for leaders to have a one-size-fits-all approach to solving their organization's problems."

"Well, that's because those people are battling immaturity. They don't have a complete toolbox," Henry explained. "If I come to a conflict and all I have is aggression, I'm going to argue my way into making people submit. But we won't have resolution. If I have a lot of fear, I'm just going to run and kind of hide and avoid it, but it's still there. You see the problem?"

Henry's explanation of incompleteness—the professional term for immaturity—made complete sense. I asked him what the solution to immaturity is, given that we're all a work in progress and we're all likely to encounter numerous instances of conflict along the path to maturity.

"We want leaders to be in a process where they're developing a complete toolbox so they don't know what they're going to do until they get in there. The Bible says he who gives an answer before he understands is a fool. In the same way, when you ask somebody, 'How do you handle conflict?' I would hope the answer is, 'With wisdom, grace, and truth.' What you don't want to hear is, 'Oh, we already know what he is going to do before he gets in there,' because that means the person is acting on autopilot, out of his or her immaturity.

"You know, the Latin word meaning 'to confront' is a very positive word. It means 'to face something frontally' or literally 'to turn your face toward something.' Now, we've given confrontation a negative connotation. We see it as adversarial or as going to battle, but all it really means is that we are going to turn and face this issue. That's a very positive thing. Confrontation just means you're facing reality, but you're doing it with grace and truth."

"So what I hear you saying is that leaders need to revise their understanding of what confrontation is all about and come to the situation with a different mind-set," I said, sounding like a psychologist practicing active listening with a patient. Henry nodded and continued.

"Right, leaders need to learn skills for dealing with conflict and to find out that confrontation can be good. And it's important for leaders to remember that they get what they tolerate. There's no such thing as effective leadership without the ability to confront well, so it's very important that they get past that."

Henry might have said more, but I was captivated by the idea that "you get what you tolerate." I sat there remembering certain situations where problems brewed unnecessarily, simply because I'd tolerated silliness for too long. By the time I confronted the matter, it was a raging issue. I shook my head in disbelief at my own failures in this area and then locked into what he was saying next.

"On the other end of the continuum, if conflict comes too easily, then that means you don't really understand how hard it is for some people to be confronted. These are people who have lost touch with the experience of fear, vulnerability, and hurt. They are potential train wrecks to the organization because they have the probability of doing conflict poorly." I assumed he stopped describing the harsh end of the continuum because he recognized that engaging in conflict too easily was not my problem.

You get what you tolerate.

"So confrontation," he said, changing his posture as if to signal the end of our impromptu private consultation, "is one of the most important things that a leader does. The result of good confrontation is that it contains toxicity, chaos, problems, and fear and quarantines them. Another way to say this is that a leader's ability to confront is the immune system of the organization. If the organization doesn't have a good immune system, then there's probably disease everywhere. Or, if the leader handles confrontation poorly, then the organization has an autoimmune disease where it's eating its own body. Getting this right is really, really important."

By this time, John Townsend had wandered over to our secluded area and listened in on the last few minutes of the conversation. Henry filled him in on what we were talking about, and John briefly added his thoughts.

"My advice about conflict is that you'd better make it normal ASAP, because if you don't make conflict a norm—something you expect, have adapted to, and have the skills to handle—conflict's going to get you and it will ruin, or at least negatively affect, the kind of fruit you want to bear. You know there are several types of conflict. There's conflict—"

"Whoa, whoa, put a cork in it right there, buddy," I warned Psychologist Number Two. "I already got all of that from your colleague here. You guys must drink out of the same well. I get it. Like many leaders, I have issues with conflict and I need to get whole and deal with them in a straightforward, honest, loving manner. Sheesh!" We all guffawed at my riposte and relaxed a bit. I was discovering that this conflict stuff can get a guy pretty tensed up.

I asked John if he deals with conflict issues much in his leadership coaching efforts.

"I spend a lot of time not only on conflict management, but on developing the skills for navigating through that. One of the most important things that leaders can learn is to stay neutral in conflict. You want to keep everybody as a good guy until there's a bad guy who's proven to be deceitful or irresponsible or toxic. Until that point, consider everybody a good guy. If you do that, then you become the disinfectant for all the bad things people are feeling toward each other. Conflict's not the end of the world, because the people working under you are most of the time terrified of conflict. They think that conflict will make them hated or get them fired. So if you can simply say, 'Oh yeah, conflict. Hey, let's go have lunch,' all of a sudden everybody calms down and they get back to the business of solving problems and bringing results."

It seemed that my little outburst at John before his final remarks had attracted more attention than intended. We now had a larger gathering of experts looped around us. I figured it was an opportune time to integrate the ideas and experiences of others, so I asked if there were ever times when it was reasonable or even necessary for a leader to create conflict in order to advance the organizational agenda.

Without hesitation, Henry affirmed the concept of leaders orchestrating conflict. "Absolutely. And there are also times when the leader has got to *not* confront. The interesting thing about all of this is there's an operating system of wisdom that's underneath it. Wisdom for the leader is sometimes, for a bigger purpose, overlooking something a person has done because it is in the best interest of his or her development or making a deal work. On the other hand, there are certain things that a leader must confront instantly or, as you phrased it, orchestrate. A good leader is very strategic about when to confront, how to confront, why to confront, and whom to confront."

As people mulled this over, Henry gave an example. "I was just involved in a consulting project where there was a team meeting. Conflict erupted, and one of the people on the team was just so out of line that the board of directors called an immediate meeting right after that. They chose to impose very, very severe consequences. They confronted that person immediately with those consequences because it was the kind of behavior and toxicity that could not be tolerated.

"In another instance, though, a leader may see some behavior and decide to overlook it because he or she knows the person is in a development stage and is coming along. So there are some things that you coach people through and other things that may be more serious.

"In the New Testament Paul says that you should reject a divisive person after a second warning. There's a difference between a foolish person and an evil person. Foolish people cause collateral damage. They're not trying to hurt anybody; they're just irresponsible and don't take ownership of their own issues and responsibilities. They cause a lot of chaos and disruption and other problems, but they're really not trying to. So you confront them and give them consequences and discipline and limits and all that, and sometimes you can save them. But then sometimes there are people who really have it in for a leader. They are really divisive and they like it when there's discord, so they try to stir that up. They like it when the leader fails or falls. That's the kind of person with whom confrontation is more like cutting a cancer out, and it's got to be done swiftly."

Laurie Beth Jones had been tracking with Henry's comments and added the benefit of some of her experience.

"Conflict comes with the job. Leaders are the ones who are blazing new trails and going where no one has dared to go before, so conflict is to be expected, not feared. In fact, it is sometimes something to be encouraged. Conflict and confrontation are healthy. For instance, when there's universal silence in the room around a decision, that's a good time to stir the pot. There's a tendency for certain personality types to be passive-aggressive, where they hide or mask their anger, but it will come out. Feelings go somewhere; they don't just go away, so to be able to draw that out in the individual is healthy. Also, if you are really a leader and everybody is just going along with you, you need to question that complacency. That's a time to figure out if you are really leading or if you are just running a popularity contest."

Barry Black, the Senate's chaplain, was the next person to speak. He, too, voiced his support for carefully orchestrating conflict in certain situations.

"Sometimes you have to initiate conflict, like Jesus cleansing the Temple. He had to know that this was going to hasten His execution, but He did it because it needed to be done. You have great leaders like Andrew Jackson who seemed to thrive on it. He was an individual who knew the right time to try to generate conflict and sometimes loving confrontation. That's why Ephesians 4:15 tells us to speak the truth in love.

"Sometimes you need to avoid conflict. Sometimes you can redirect it, or deflect it, or even postpone it. And, yes, sometimes it's good to orchestrate it. Frederick Douglass once said that you can't expect to get a crop without plowing, and you can't expect to see a harvest without rain and thunder and lightning. So, often, conflict is constructive.

"I was in Alabama in the '60s and participated in the desegregation of lunch counters. And that's a classic example, where we would walk in to sit at lunch counters, and the conflict was not from the police officers who would eventually come and carry us off to jail, but from the angry folk who were there, who would start fights. They were going to pull us off of the lunch counter; they were not going to wait for the law to come. Yet Martin King had us believing in the power of nonviolent redemption and in the power of this strategy, which was a mixture of Gandhi, Thoreau, and Jesus Christ, to arouse the conscience of the nation. He showed us that by orchestrating this conflict we would eventually get what we desired, and that was to have the chains of segregation and discrimination removed. And we headed for the jail singing. It was an astonishing thing. So conflict can often be used in a very constructive way."

Conflict comes with the job.

The room was quiet as we heard this dignified African American man speak about the tribulations of leadership—and how facilitating conflict had brought about significant consequences for doing the right thing, as Coach Holtz would say.

While the chaplain's recollections put most of us in a ponderous mood, his words got Erwin McManus really thinking. Erwin has a unique way of looking at things and expressing his perspective, as demonstrated by his response regarding the obligation of a leader to orchestrate conflict.

"If you're a leader, you cannot tolerate the discontinuity between what someone says and what that person does, if the two don't match. I cannot tolerate it when we pretend that we're a servant culture, and we pretend we care about people, and we pretend we care about a world drowning in poverty and disease and yet we do nothing about it. We say all that, and then nothing in our culture and in our values reflects those concerns. I just don't have any tolerance for that. And so I realize that I don't just find conflict, I guess I create conflict. When I think about Paul of Tarsus, whom many historians call the founder of Christianity due to his enormous influence, everywhere he went he found danger. I keep reading about it and I think, *I have a feeling those places were safe before he got there. And maybe even safe after he left.* I think Paul brought the danger with him. And I think leadership is about bringing the danger with you."

I laughed out loud at that statement, perhaps inappropriately—okay, I was the only one laughing at it, so it was undoubtedly inappropriate. But I couldn't help myself. *It was so blasted brilliant.* Most of us—including me—would have stated a similar idea, but more softly: "Leaders make people uncomfortable. We take them out of their comfort zones." But Erwin pushed the boundary: leaders bring danger within the arc of their shadow because they diligently seek the truth, they unfailingly tell the truth, and they won't settle for anything less than the truth. And when a leader performs at that level, it can get uncomfortable. Sometimes it even demands confrontation. Any leader who is that sold out to doing what is right, to seeking truth—that's a dangerous person. But it's also a person who will transform the world, because nothing can stand in his or her way.

I had to take a seat. That thought was worth the price of admission for me. But while we had a captive crowd that was now fully engaged in this subject, we had to push the ball downfield. So I acknowledged the value of using conflict as a tool to make progress, but asked how the process of resolving conflict works. Ben Carson offered some ideas on that topic.

"You must take the initiative. You cannot be passive, because the conflict will just continue to escalate and metastasize. It needs to be recognized and snuffed out—not necessarily with an authoritarian hand, but often with insight therapy, which works extremely well."

He stopped speaking. I squinted at him, as I do sometimes when I'm baffled, and asked him what insight therapy is.

"Insight therapy," he patiently explained, "is where you get the conflicting parties to analyze why they feel the way they do and get them to understand that perhaps there are different avenues for resolving this conflict than the confrontation they have chosen."

While I was chewing on that concept, Miles McPherson provided another idea that proved to be helpful.

"When I have a conflict with somebody, I have learned that asking questions for clarification and giving people the opportunity to clarify their position often lessens the conflict and brings people together. I have learned to come into a confrontation with smiles and to tell the people involved that I just want to clarify the situation. I want to be sure that I don't offend them and to remember that a soft answer turns away wrath. You can win a friend by giving somebody the benefit of the doubt while at the same time clarifying what went wrong, and perhaps avoiding direct conflict. In the end, the goal is to walk out of there rejoicing that we really fixed the problem. Some people look at conflict as having to win a fight versus wanting to fix a problem. Those are two different things. If you go into the discussion feeling like you just want to fix the problem, then you will go about it differently than if you go in believing you have to be right and you have to win the fight."

Leaders bring danger within the arc of their shadow because they diligently seek the truth, they unfailingly tell the truth, and they won't settle for anything less than the truth.

I mentioned that it seemed as if we were dancing around the concept of negotiation as one of the tools that Henry had talked about in the beginning of this conversation. Barry picked up on that theme.

"In negotiation, one of the things that we often fail to do is to engage in the requisite research before we actually negotiate. You really need to have done your homework so that you do not enter the negotiation process without adequate knowledge. It's like going to buy a new car without having any idea what the dealer paid for the car. That's silly. So you've got to do the requisite research. But second, you have to listen, because very often you can discover where the boundaries are and what the needs of the individual with whom you're negotiating are. The same strategy you use in the leadership development process, where you listen in order to learn to lead, is something you need to do in negotiating as well."

As Barry spoke, I was again impressed by how often listening had been mentioned as a critical leadership skill. So many of the tasks that a leader needs to perform—from developing vision to hiring, from developing trust to creating shared values, and from creating a healthy culture to resolving conflict—depend upon good listening.

"Third, it's important to strive for a win-win scenario. If the individual you're negotiating with doesn't win, you haven't won. Eliminate the win-lose scenario from your slate of options."

To me that factor sounded like rhetoric, not reality. I mentioned as much to Barry and asked him if there are practical ways to make the pursuit of a win-win outcome more probable. He cited me for jumping the gun; his next point would address that matter.

"Fourth, you've got to be creative. Too many of us engage in dichotomous thinking and we are not aware of the multiplicity of nuances. Often, some healthy brainstorming will enable you to come up with something that's unorthodox but maybe extremely successful in the negotiation process.

"Fifth, being patient is a critical factor. You have to be patient enough to be willing to walk away. Many times it's when I'm walking away that I'm called back, so patience is invaluable.

"And then finally, a critical part of negotiating is to trust God for favor."

Barry made this statement so unassumingly that it sounded simple and natural. But for many of us, trusting God is a concept we embrace but don't always practice. It was helpful for Barry to have made that the capstone of the process.

Having received all of this valuable input, I turned to look at Henry, who had hung in there through this entire journey. I asked him if he had any final thoughts on the issue before I had to scoot back to the stage to transition to the next speaker.

He reiterated what had been said about listening, about being open minded enough to consider options beyond those you embraced when entering the negotiations, and about truly desiring a positive outcome for everyone. Then he introduced a good thought as our end point.

"One aspect we haven't really touched on is being able to tell people your understanding. Don't go into a negotiation and say, 'What's important to us is this,' or 'What we need from you is A, B, and C.' Begin with, 'Okay, now as I understand things, and as I listen to you, it seems that what you really need in this situation is this and that, and what would be most helpful for your purposes are these other particulars. That's what I am hearing from you. Do I have that right?' Once they know that your intent is to understand their needs and to meet those to the best of your ability, then at some point it's a lot easier for you to say, 'You know, in doing this, would it be okay with you if I try to work out an arrangement for such and such?'

"In negotiation, what you're trying to do, among other things, is to avoid a fight-or-flight syndrome. The brain is always scanning in milliseconds to figure out if what is coming at it is friend or foe. If the brain feels like what it's encountering is either neutral or foe, then you're one millisecond away from the person going into fight or flight. What that means is, they're either moving away from your position or they're going to be against it, so you've got to remove anything in what you're doing that puts matters into an adversarial position or that makes them think that their interest is not your interest. When people realize that you're really there to meet their needs in the best way that you can, then all sorts of magic can happen between you."

And I guess that's what all of us leaders really want, isn't it: the magic that can get everyone on the same page, moving together toward a shared vision that facilitates positive transformation. Who knew that conflict could be one of the tools or conditions that would bring such life change to pass?

CHAPTER 10

CHARACTER

I RETURNED TO THE VENUE on day two of the event refreshed and ready for another mind-boggling day. After the discussion about conflict I'd closed the day's proceedings and returned to the hotel, my head swimming with information, ideas, and challenges. It felt like grad school compressed into thirty-six hours. And I felt like the most fortunate person on earth to have such a mentoring intensive.

Upon reviewing the day's schedule, I noted that in between the onstage appearance and a workshop I had to do, there were five more greenroom slots. During the night I had charted the course of yesterday's conversations, evaluated the topics covered, and figured today would be the day to fill in the obvious holes. I was reviewing a note card on which I'd written some possible discussion topics when John Townsend came alongside of me, a cup of coffee in hand, and put his arm around me.

"I know what you're doing," he said with a grin. When people say something like that to me, half the time *I* don't know what I'm doing and I wish they'd just straighten me out. He continued, "And I think it's great. One of the conversation starters you throw into the mix today might have to do with character. I think we've talked about some really vital elements of leadership back here, but I'd hate for us not to get centered by recognizing the importance of the leader's character."

Now this was outstanding. Not only was I being so transparent that everyone knew exactly what I was doing, they were also excited enough about it to help form the process. What? I'm not fooling you either? Okay, a more realistic way of positioning this is that I was so obviously needy as a leader that everyone was aware of it, and they took pity on my sorry self and were trying to guide me to places I was so misguided about that I didn't even realize those subjects needed to be on my radar. Happy?

Whatever the case, I was very pleased that John had raised character as a viable topic for discussion. I asked him how he would start out such a conversation.

"Character is important to focus on in the sense that who you are will determine how successful you are over time. A while back, I began spending more and more of my work time with leaders in the corporate world as well as with leaders in the pastoral world. I kept seeing that the winners were people who had certain very strong character attributes that were consistent over time and formed a pattern. And I saw that the losers—the ones who weren't meeting goals, or were burned out, or did not succeed over time— were the ones who did not have the necessary character attributes."

As had become the pattern, a group of people who had straggled in for the morning sessions were now gathered around us. One of them was Patrick Lencioni, one of the best imitations of the Energizer Bunny I'd ever met. He is high energy morning, noon, and night. But he also has such a wonderful, consistent perspective on leadership that you can understand why he is always "up." He threw his two cents on character into the ring, challenging a common perception about the entire leadership endeavor.

"Leadership is not about skill. It's about character. Too often we hire a leader for an organization because he or she has experience in the industry. But think about it: a person can learn the industry in months, but if that person doesn't have the character, you are going to have to hire the local minister and priest and Dr. Phil for twelve years of therapy! Don't you think you need to look first at character?"

Patrick was preaching to the choir now. "With leadership in any position, I look at character first. In my own company, even when I hire people for jobs that are mostly about getting things done, I look for character first, because people can learn the skills and industry-specific things that they'll need."

John appreciated Patrick's line of thought and picked up the baton. "When people look at character they sometimes think, *Oh, you mean somebody who doesn't cheat on his income taxes and who's faithful to his spouse,* and all that. That's certainly part of it, but character is much more than just the fact that you're a moral person with good values. Character is essentially the set of abilities you need to meet the demands of life. In the Greek language, *character* means your experiences. It refers to your internal makeup, so character also includes how well you relate to others. People with good character are able to extend their hearts and reach other people's hearts and let other people into their hearts.

Leadership is not about skill. It's about character.

"Character is also about how you deal with failure," John continued. "Are you able to accept failure and realize you're not perfect? Can you be open about that, or do you always want to be the good guy? Can you accept imperfections in others? When I'm working with a leader, character is one of the first things I look at, examining the insides to see if the machine is tuned up."

I appreciated all that had been said but was confused by something John had alluded to regarding values. When he said that character is more than being "a moral person with good values," did that mean values are an insignificant part of character?

"No, not at all. As I observed successful leaders, there were several attributes that kept coming up. And one was that they have a clear sense of healthy values. Values like being honest, or believing that doing it the hard way is worth it, or thinking that people are important. These successful leaders were defined by their values, and these were the right values."

It's probably the researcher in me, always wanting to count and categorize everything, but I felt a compulsion to have the experts identify what matters in character. I knew from my own work with leaders that the Bible identifies more than fifty different character traits that honor God. But in this milieu I wanted to know which of those traits stood out as especially indispensable for those who would lead people.

Mike Huckabee, genial and warm even in the morning, kicked off that discussion by reminding us that consistency is critical. "The best definition of character is that it is those qualities that make you the person you are when nobody else is looking. So character is that which causes you to make the same decision in public that you would make in private."

I found that interesting in light of the political scene. How many instances of public rhetoric have failed to parallel the private behavior of our political leaders? I raised the issue and asked if someone could be a good public leader despite a questionable private life. Before Mike could answer, Newt Gingrich, his fellow Republican, responded.

"Who you are inevitably shapes who you are. Can you be a total scoundrel in private but a terrific public leader? No—at least not very often. On the other hand every leader we've ever had—including Abraham Lincoln and George Washington and Franklin Roosevelt, who I think are the greatest leaders we've ever had—is a human being. So I'm never shocked when people sin, because my understanding of Christ's teaching is that sin is the inevitable behavior of everyone."

So if we grant that none of us is perfect but that character is crucial to our ability to lead people successfully, then what are the most important character attributes for leaders to focus upon and to be consistent with?

John answered my question. "Going back to my observations of successful leaders, I found that they really wanted to connect on a personal level with people, which basically meant listening. They were good listeners. A lot of leaders who are good communicators communicate the vision and what they want, and that's important. But I found that the differential was the ones who could listen when people were disappointed in them and when people had different ideas than they did, and were able to understand the other point of view. They tended to draw people out who had problems that couldn't be solved, and they didn't gloss over the bad news. They really connected with the difficult stuff people were dealing with."

Hearing that, my interpretation was that great leaders are intentional about establishing and nurturing relationships with people, because they care about those people. I floated that idea and got a response from Sam Chand.

"One of the nonnegotiable elements of a leader's character is how he or she treats others. It goes back to that recurring theme of caring for people. I have seen leaders walking through the office, past different people they think of as flunkies or gofers. If a leader has high respect for people—all people, regardless of their positions—then I know that I can work with this person. But if a leader has low respect for people, that tells me how that person views people, and that's a whole other issue."

Sam's thoughts sparked a memory for Erwin McManus, which he shared with us.

"I was just in a studio with directors, writers, editors, and postproduction people for a film we've been making. The most talented and accredited person in the room was the most deferring. After we reviewed a clip he said, 'If you guys don't like this, then you know, we'll just start from scratch. We'll just start all over again.' Now, he was the only one in the whole room who had been nominated for an Academy Award. But I saw no one else relenting except for him. And I'll be honest with you: I would rather just sit and listen to that guy. I admire that. The person who has the most right to wield power just released it and acted as if he was thinking, *Okay, what can I do to bring everybody into this and to help you accomplish your dream?*

"Somewhere along the way, I began admiring people who have that kind of humility. I wanted to be like them and longed to become that kind of person. And then, on a practical, gritty level, I thought, *Look, I don't know how to be humble, but I know how to do humble things. So I'm just going to fake it.*"

His honesty caused us all to laugh.

"*I'm just going to take out the garbage and stack the chairs and clean the floor and scrub some toilets. That's what all the people I really admire do, and maybe, eventually, it will translate into who I am.* I think we have to actually love humility. And that's how you can begin to know if you're moving in that direction: when you love people who live lives of humility, people who are self-effacing, and people who are deferential."

"I think you're describing something that I've thought of as important in character, and that's selflessness," added Rich Stearns. "People want a leader whom they perceive is not out for him- or herself. They are looking for someone who recognizes that it's not about me, the leader; it's about you and it's about the mission and it's about the team. It's not about me."

A series of sidebar exchanges erupted after Rich finished. As those died down, John Ashcroft offered an addendum to Rich's thoughts on selflessness, putting the concept in a different light.

"You have to have a dimension beyond yourself, but it doesn't mean you have to be selfless. You can have a high opinion of yourself, but you also have to have a dimension that is about things other than yourself. It is more noble to be willing to sacrifice yourself for others and for a cause if you realize you are worth something and have value than if you think you are a piece of dirt and you don't have value. The Bible doesn't say you shouldn't think well of yourself. It says you shouldn't think better of yourself than you do of others. You have to have a dimension that is beyond self."

This had become a very intense and interesting discussion. These were the people who modeled great leadership for millions of leaders around the world. Getting inside their heads on the issue of character was proving to be a fascinating exercise. And the interaction between Rich's and John's words showed that similar ideas sometimes become tangled up in differences of language. Clearly, both men concurred that no matter what you call it, a great leader is one whose character allows him or her to get over him- or herself and realize that we lead for the benefit of others. The comments that followed underscored this realization.

With a warm smile toward General Ashcroft, Rich offered more of his thinking about character.

"I also think the best leaders have a very keen sense of self-awareness. They take account of how they are perceived by others, how their words are received by others, what their blind spots and weaknesses are, and what their strengths are. If you're self-aware in all of those areas, you have a much stronger ability to know what impact you're having on people and you know what things you need to compensate for in your own personality and abilities."

Someone asked Rich if he had observed any effective leaders who lack such self-awareness.

"I've seen leaders who are not self-aware," he admitted, "and they're almost like blind people, constantly bumping into things because they don't see them. They have a terrible time navigating through their jobs because they don't realize the impact they're having on others. They might be grossly micromanaging others, but they don't see it. The people who work for them are terribly frustrated, but these people can't seem to get their boss to understand that he or she needs to give them more space and stop micromanaging them. Leaders who are not self-aware will say things in meetings that are hurtful to people, without even realizing that they are hurting people."

Another question was raised about what you can do to help such a person.

"That lack of self-awareness is very hard to deal with in performance reviews," Rich replied. "You see, perception is reality. If I go to a meeting with one of my leaders and I say, 'You've got to stop micromanaging people. You're stifling and smothering people. You're trying to do their jobs for them,' they say,

The best leaders have a very keen sense of self-awareness.

'No, I'm not. I'm not like that. I don't do that. I don't micromanage. I don't know what you're talking about.' And my answer is, 'You know what? Perception is reality. I'm telling you that you're perceived as micromanaging everyone. And whether you believe it or not, that's the way you're being perceived. So you've either got to change the perception or the reality, but either way, you've got to deal with it because it's undermining your ability to lead.'

"So I think self-awareness is a crucial characteristic," stated Rich, as he summarized his thoughts. "We've all seen this in our families. We've all got a crazy aunt or uncle or sister or brother who just doesn't get it. They don't see the impact they have on others; they don't realize how inappropriate some of the things they say are in a family gathering. Often, it's because they just don't have a sense of who they are or the impact of their behavior."

John Townsend, who had initiated this line of thinking, connected the most recent ideas to another element in a leader's character.

"I also observed that successful leaders have a high sense of responsibility over their lives. At the end of the day, they take accountability for the successes and the failures. They have zero tolerance for blaming and zero tolerance for excuses. In that respect, they are harder on themselves than they are on others. Because of that they are able to achieve more; they are in control of their lives, and they believe they have made the choices in their lives.

"Conversely, they are good at being clearly defined. That means they do not take responsibility for things they shouldn't take responsibility for. So you won't see them micromanage and do someone else's job because they think they can do it better. They know how to let things go. They also don't take responsibility for someone else's negative feelings. They don't run around trying to make everybody like them all the time."

That was another entire subject that I would pursue later: the issues of pressure, popularity, and criticism. But John had reinforced Rich's point about having responsibility and accountability as part of one's character composition. To complete his train of thought, John gave us one more observation about character from his work with leaders.

"Finally, I also noticed that they are well versed in failure and comfortable with failure. That enables them to take risks, to be creative, and to learn, because failure is the key to those things, and they have very little sense of shame or guilt or embarrassment or negative self-talk about failing. There are certainly people who are more gifted and talented in those areas than others, but that in no way means that every single leader cannot also have a clear set of healthy values, be able to listen to and connect emotionally with others, be clear on what he or she is and isn't responsible for, and be a person who welcomes and learns from failure."

The group gave John a hearty round of encouragement. It was clear that character matters, and these leaders had worked hard on honing their character and took it seriously in those whom they hired and worked with. So it seemed inevitable that once the afterglow from John's comments subsided, others would offer additional traits to consider.

Successful leaders have a high sense of responsibility over their lives.

I was not disappointed. Soon enough, Mike Huckabee kept the conversation alive with thoughts on an attribute that was sure to be raised eventually: integrity.

"You've got to be honest with yourself and with God. A great leader must demonstrate honesty, based on a code of internal honor. Being hated and losing but being able to live with yourself because you were honest is far better than winning but not being able to live with yourself."

"Ah, I find that so many leaders have a hard time telling the story the same way each time, you know?" said Sam Chand. "They embellish stuff. And when they do, that casts a shadow, and I wonder how much of what they say is really true. I'm also looking for them to keep their promises. If they say that we are going to do certain things, I never take anyone's promise at face value. I ask them, 'Are you sure about this?' I nail them down to it because part of character is keeping your word. I have no problem with people changing their minds. But pick up the phone, e-mail, text, and tell me that you changed your mind. I'm good with that."

"I am a true believer that people want to follow leaders with integrity, leaders they trust, leaders they respect, leaders they admire for the character of their lives and the integrity of their lives," was the vigorous acknowledgment from Rich. "They want their leaders to have integrity in every dimension: in their marriages, as parents, in their communities, with their finances—not just integrity in the workplace.

"I've had bosses who lacked integrity, and I just didn't want to get up every morning and go to work, because I didn't want to serve someone like that. Those kinds of people don't inspire me, first of all. I'm always cynical about their motives, assuming they're just in it for themselves and feeling unable to believe anything they say.

"Unfortunately many leaders who lack integrity compensate by using fear. They figure, *Well, they don't like me, but I'll make them afraid of me.* That's another way to lead, but it's not a good way to do it."

I was pleased that Michael Franzese seized on Rich's observation about leading through fear because as a former Mafia boss, Michael had relied on fear as a leadership tool for years. Having since been imprisoned and, more importantly, having accepted Christ and completely reformed his way of thinking about life and leadership, Michael provided some hard-won insights into the dangers of leading through intimidation.

"When I was growing up, I idolized my dad," he said, referring to one of the top leaders in the Colombo crime family in New York. "I wanted to emulate him and his life. He was powerful and respected and looked up to. I noticed that my dad was a gentleman, that he treated people the right way and garnered their respect. But as I grew up and had greater understanding, I saw that fear was a big factor. Now fear is not a factor in how I lead. Now it's more about respect and love. If people respect and love me, then my leadership becomes stronger."

It's one of the fascinating facts of life that when a former mob leader speaks, people listen. Americans, perhaps due to the mystique created by the Godfather movies, are riveted by inside looks at what really happens behind the scenes in the world of organized crime. Michael is perhaps the only significant figure from that world to have told the truth, done hard time, and walked away to live a clean and productive life after years in the underworld. His story is compelling, but not as much as the person he has become. He offered a few more nuggets of wisdom for us.

"In my life before, I saw people who led without integrity, and it always caught up to them because they relied on fear and intimidation. Today I understand that integrity and honesty are very important. You see, it's one thing to be a boss, but it's another thing to be a leader. People want to see something in you that makes them trust in you, that makes them want to go to the mat with you. They want to believe that what you say is true. Your track record is extremely important, because people look at that and they trust you based on it. You want them to follow you based on that trust, not based on fear."

As people thanked Michael for his contribution, we continued discussing matters of character. Rich said there were three other qualities he wanted to put on the table as requirements.

"First, people want a fair leader. Second, they want a leader who has empathy—you know, as Bill Clinton would say, one who feels their pain. The leader gets it and understands their points of pain and can relate to them in substantial ways. And people want a leader who understands and practices forgiveness. We want to follow someone who forgives others and who asks to be forgiven when he or she has made a mistake. Leaders often don't ask for forgiveness, and it can have a very powerful effect in an organization."

Rich stopped for a moment, pursed his lips, and furrowed his brow, then gave a quick story about the power of forgiveness in leadership. "We had a big meeting not too long ago. We've had some real organizational problems in the last couple of years with our major-donor fund-raising group, which produced some changes in leadership. There has been a lot of discontent. We had a high-level summit meeting to try to determine how to best address these issues. Early on I told the group, 'You know what? As CEO of World Vision, my greatest failure over the last ten years has been a failure to serve this function well. I have put the wrong people in the jobs, and I have failed to solve the problems that need to be solved to make you successful. As I look back at those ten years, I look at this as one of my greatest failures, and therefore I commit to you today that I want to give this a very high priority. I want to make this work for you, to make this better.'

"Well, that changed the whole tenor of the meeting. Their reaction was like, 'Really?' You have to be willing to take responsibility and, if necessary, to seek the forgiveness of the people you have not served well. It turned that meeting from a cynical gripe fest into a productive time where people were asking, 'How can we fix this? How can we join together to make this work?' But it had to start with me saying, 'You know, I'm not perfect and I've done some things to mess this up, and I'm sorry.'"

As people congratulated Rich for "being a big boy" and admitting his imperfections to those he leads, someone described his actions as a demonstration of courage and wisdom. We had not yet discussed wisdom as a critical character trait, but the consensus was that it is, indeed, important for leaders. Newt had some thoughts about getting the wisdom required to lead well.

"Wisdom is something you have to allow to come to you. You cannot acquire it. You can go out and become smart, but you have to open yourself up and listen to inner voices before wisdom can come to you. Adam Smith argues that there's a man in the mirror and that we are inherently moral, which is why the Scottish Enlightenment said pursuit of happiness is wisdom and virtue. Wisdom is what's left after all the other stuff disappears."

With the first session of the day nearing the start time and the speakers getting their heads wrapped around their contribution to today's event, we finished up with a very incisive perspective from Lou Taylor.

"Almost all of the opportunities where I've really been able to lead in an effective manner have been birthed or granted out of an absolute willingness to submit. Sometimes that has meant submitting to people who were obviously not godly, but to nevertheless submit and be patient. I think that has probably been my greatest revelation about leadership, that the ability to lead comes from character development within myself first.

"People perceive submission as a weakness, but I think there is no greater strength than to truly submit and be patient until there's an absolute understanding, an absolute knowledge, or an opportunity that allows you to rise to the occasion and lead. Sometimes you're not given that opportunity, but your character is being revealed in the midst of that, and the willingness to take a backseat sometimes gives you the opportunities to lead.

"I'm in a situation where we manage so many people's personal lives and careers, but although we're making decisions on a daily basis, there's almost always a team approach or other professionals involved in perpetuating somebody's career or financial well-being. When you're in a position of making those kinds of decisions, sometimes your desire to be the primary leader is not granted. Sometimes you're an oarsman, sometimes you're on the lookout, and sometimes you're the captain. Submission is vital."

Perhaps Lou's comments at the end of our time best summarized what I needed to take away from this excursion into character development. If I, as a leader, am exposed to the needs of the people I've been called to lead and remain sensitive to the concerns that emerge in my conscience, God will reveal the areas of my character that need to be refined. Based on personal experience, I had no doubt that He would also be happy to participate in that refining process. As one of my colleagues had mentioned, character development is an ongoing, never-ending process.

So let the journey continue.

CHAPTER 11

FOLLOWING

THE DAY WAS OFF to a great start. Our speakers were feeling enthusiastic about what we were doing, the audience was showing their appreciation in various ways, and the leaders were having a good time with each other off-stage. I had learned long ago that leadership is a tough job and can become a lonely occupation. For that reason, I had observed that in a conference setting, leaders are generally quite comfortable in the presence of other leaders. They don't have to take care of each other, they don't have to answer to each other, and they easily resonate with the language, experiences, challenges, and joys that they all share. And sure enough, as I reentered the greenroom, I found the place buzzing with conversation.

I made a beeline to one of the food tables, stocked up on a few breakfast items and a cup of tea, then moseyed over to a gathering that was ignoring the monitor in favor of a conversation already in progress. As I walked up, I heard Rich Stearns speaking.

"Before he died I had a chance to spend a day with Peter Drucker. He made a statement I never forgot. He said, 'Everybody writes books about leadership. Somebody ought to write a book about followership, because for every leader there are a thousand followers.' He was kind of saying, 'Enough about leadership. Let's teach people to be followers.' He didn't really elaborate on that, but I always thought it was a good idea."

I thought it was a good idea, too. John Kotter had some concerns, though, about the very topic.

"I don't know a whole lot of leaders who have taught much about followers. I think they would see that as somehow condescending—do you understand what I mean? Their view would be that these are not followers, they're people. It's not *them*, it's *we*. It's not 'me leader, you follower.' I don't think great leaders think in those terms."

So that set off a healthy discussion about semantics and perceptions. We emerged from it with General Bob Dees. His years leading in the military (army), business (Microsoft), and ministry (Campus Crusade for Christ) had allowed him to view leadership from multiple angles. As he'd jokingly said to me in a prior conversation, he'd seen it all.

"Some leaders are easy to follow; others are not. The ones who are easy to follow are the ones who are fairly accepting of others as people, and accepting of failure or substandard performance in the right way. In those cases, people are able to perceive that the leader has their best interests at heart. In playing this out, you have to see if the leader makes time to coach the follower so the follower improves, and if the leader affirms the follower sufficiently when the follower's output is positive.

"What the leader is really doing is setting the conditions for the next decision or event. That very first decision defines the character of the commander, because the follower is still trying to figure it out. The leader makes it easier for the follower if he or she sets the conditions for dialogue, affirmation, and coaching. Having established that climate between the leader and the led, he or she becomes a person that people want to follow."

What Bob had said made sense, but it raised the question of what it takes to create that kind of climate.

"One of the elements is competence," he noted. "People will follow more aggressively if they understand their role, so establishing a division of labor and clear boundaries is important. A wise leader is able to craft mutually exclusive and collectively exhaustive relationships across his or her team, meaning that he or she covers all the bases without inappropriately covering the same base multiple times for no good reason.

"Another principle is that things break at the seams. So the wise leader knows that as you're instructing your followers and making it easier for them to respond and support, you not only define a good division of labor, but gain a bit of altitude so you can monitor the seams. The leader must look at the interface between organizations, and between individuals of dissimilar functions, which then allows you to take the sand out of the gears so that followers have clarity and are not precluded from realizing their purpose."

Bob's comments brought Ken Melrose back to an experience he'd had at Toro. His narrative was an example of the value of empathy based on understanding what those in the rank and file needed and perceived.

"We had a plant that was unionized, and we knew that they didn't trust management. I went down to the plant one day and I wanted to walk around. So the plant manager and the head of the union and I walked up and down the assembly lines. The union steward was upset because the plant manager kept increasing the line rates for productivity, which was a fair thing to do, to increase productivity, but he pushed back on me and asked, 'Would you tell your plant manager to slow the lines down? You're not getting the kind of quality you want because we have to make the lawn mowers too fast.'

"Well, that gave me an idea. I said to him, 'Come on, Emil. I could bring my management team from Minneapolis down here and make these line rates.' And he got red in the face and started poking me, and then he challenged me. 'Yeah, you bring your management team down here and show us how you can make these line rates.' So I kind of set us up for failure—which was exactly what I wanted to do! I wanted our management team to come down and try to do what the plant people were doing, and just see that they couldn't do it and that the plant people who were really good at what they did couldn't either.

"So here we were all over the plant, about twenty of us, working side by side with the plant people, trying to put these lawn mowers together. There were these buttons that we could hit to stop the line, and they would make a yellow flash. I'll tell you, those lights were going off all over the place. It looked like Christmas. The plant manager or the foreman would yell out, 'What's wrong?' and somebody would yell back, 'Oh, nothing. Management couldn't keep up. They made some mistakes.' So they'd slow the line down and then they'd slow it down some more. We got to demonstrate that we were not very good at that.

"We learned something else during that process too. We noticed all the plant people just jabbering and talking while they were putting the mowers together. During our turn, I was frantically trying to do the job, and I said to them, 'Don't talk. I'm concentrating.' But I could hear what they were saying to each other. They were talking about raising money for the church, or coaching Little League, or dealing with an illness, or helping with some tragedy. We had a postmortem meeting with some of the plant people, and one of our management people said, 'It's really interesting. I never thought about this, but you all have the same issues that my wife and I have. She's trying to raise money for our church, and I'm a Little League coach, and my mother is very sick and in the hospital. You know, you're kind of like us.' To that manager it was a great revelation. All of a sudden, he was thinking, *Hey, these people are like us. And they're really good at what they do.*

"So when we met after that whole experience, we were able to say, 'Next time we need to cut costs or raise the line speed, we're going to do it in a way that values the line workers, because we don't want to lose these people and we don't want to fight with them. Let's make it right for them.' We experienced a new attitude among the management in Minneapolis.

Instead of thinking about them as 'the blue-collar people' or 'those people down in Windom,' we shifted to thinking of them as part of us. It was no longer 'them' and 'us.' Now we thought of them as part of the Toro family; they were just working in a different location. It was amazing how differently our operations and plant management people started thinking about the people in the union. It's about trusting and valuing and empowering, and having our managers recognize that everyone is important."

It seemed that the lesson Ken's group had learned was that people become better teammates when they feel as if they belong on the team and are accepted by the leaders as being a vital part of the team.

"There's no doubt about it," Ken responded. "If somebody's sick in a line worker's family, somebody in Minneapolis goes down to help, and people in Minneapolis write letters of support. I stayed in contact with the people whom I worked with on the line. I'd write letters to Jennifer, one of the women on the line, and she'd write me back, saying, 'I never thought that I'd write a letter to the head of the company, sharing what's happening to my daughter.' It's all part of trying to make their lives better because you love them. When you build that kind of relationship, you don't have to say, 'You'd better perform or else,' because they will. They'll outperform any standard you have set because they want to."

The issue of feeling known and appreciated was something that John Townsend had seen in his leadership coaching and counseling over the years.

"At the end of the day, people need to feel like they are valuable and they are valued. That's where encouragement comes in. Only the leader can provide that. When a peer gives you encouragement it doesn't have nearly the impact as affirmation from the person who operates at fifty thousand feet above sea level and says, 'I'm glad you're with us; you are such a valuable addition to our team.' People often take a position with less benefits and money because of the encouragement factor."

A bunch of us acknowledged the importance of such encouragement but admitted that it's not a natural thing for many leaders to provide. Yet most of us enjoy that kind of affirmation when we receive it, so why is it so hard to give? We talked about being too busy to do so, or having goals that are a moving target and therefore cause current production to always seem inadequate. But John thought there was more to it than that.

"I think giving that kind of encouragement probably takes a couple of skill sets. One is the ability to obey the Golden Rule: treat others as you would like to be treated. If a leader can turn the tables in his or her interaction with a direct report or a peer or whomever and think, *What would I need if I was talking to me right now?* then it helps the leader to realize that the person he or she is talking to might need a lot of truth and feedback, yes, but what that person *really* needs is somebody to simply say, 'I'm on your team.'

"The second thing is that people need to know that they matter. They need to hear that the leader believes the workplace would be a different— not as good—setting if they were gone. People are so afraid that if they left, nobody would notice or care. But if you are able to convey to them that you depend on them being there, and it's not just what they provide but who they are as people, that's meaningful encouragement."

The general sentiment was that providing those kinds of uplifting, grateful words is a significant means of helping people follow a leader more efficiently. Wilson Goode suggested that it is not just motivational words that matter, but that people's performance is also bolstered by clear information.

"I found that the most effective way to have good followers is to inform them about where things stand. When I was mayor, and even before that, when I was a commissioner on the state's Public Utilities Commission, I held town meetings all the time. I went out, took the budget, and said, 'I want you to know how your money is being spent. Here is where the money comes from, here is where it goes, and here is what I want to do in the coming year.' I found that providing citizens with information increased their support of my leadership, and even increased the passion with which they supported what I was doing, because they had been able to come in, ask questions, and see what was going on and how things operated."

John responded that in addition to information about how things work, knowledge about what the leader expects of them will enable people to follow a leader more effectively. "If you look at the Gallup research, Marcus Buckingham makes a real strong case that the best leaders are those whose followers say they know clearly what is expected of them and who are resourced specifically to meet those expectations. They are happy because they have structure. So to help people become better followers means letting them know, not in some vague way but in a very specific, direct way, what is expected and required of them, and to resource them with the time, money, and training that they need to do those things."

As we kibitzed about how leaders might communicate such supportive thoughts to our colleagues, Sam Chand recommended communicating at an LCD level. "Make it simple. Break it down into concrete communication. Tell them the basic facts they need to know very simply: give the who, what, when, how, where. Keep everything real—real simple. Don't try to dazzle followers with the process you have come through, and don't try to impress them with your deep thinking. Just tell them what needs to happen, how it needs to happen, and when it needs to happen so that anyone can easily grasp that without losing any focus or attention."

But how do you take people who are generally abstract communicators and get them to convey vision, goals, values, plans, and the like in concrete language?

"Re-languaging is a big part of what a leader must do when he or she works with followers. In general, leaders are more abstract than concrete and followers are more concrete than abstract. A leader can often be both, but a follower can usually operate only at a concrete level. The danger is that the more education leaders get, the more their language disconnects from their followers. It's only natural: they are reading at a different level, communicating with other leaders at a different level, and writing at a different level every day. But they must remember when they go into a meeting with their followers to communicate at a level that connects with those people."

Rich Stearns had been quietly absorbing all that was being said. He seemed ready to give birth to his ideas regarding the development of effective followers. I asked him what he was thinking about.

"I tend to think about the kind of followers a leader wants on his or her team, and I've decided that as a leader you want people who are unselfish and are not pressing their own agendas.

The best leaders are those whose followers say they know clearly what is expected of them and that are resourced specifically to meet those expectations.

They come to every meeting saying, 'How can I help? How can I be of help to the team for the greater good?' You want people who are willing to do anything that you ask them to do if it will be helpful to the overall mission of the organization. But in the corporate world and even in the ministry world there tend to be more people who are approaching every meeting from their own self-interests. They're looking to find out 'What's in it for me?' and 'How will this better position me?' and 'Will I get credit for this if I do it?'

"So I always ask employees when I'm with them one-on-one, 'What kind of person would you want on your staff?' Obviously you want the one who says, 'I'm willing to do anything that you need me to do to help the team win. I don't care if it's a dirty job or a thankless job; if that's what you need me to do for the team to win, send me there. I'll do it.' Those are the kinds of people that we, as leaders, want on our team—not spineless people, but people with the willingness to help and the attitude that it's not all about them.

"But you don't want someone who blindly follows," Rich warned. "You don't want yes-men. You want people who might disagree with you and with each other, respectfully and appropriately. We make better decisions that way. Leaders who surround themselves with adoring acolytes and believe their own press clippings lose touch with reality. So surround yourself with followers who are willing to challenge.

"What that requires the leader to do, though, is to invite people to do that, because a leader's position is imposing. When I'm in a meeting, especially when it's with people who are two or three levels below me, I'm always very careful to say, 'Here's an idea. And please, I want you to understand that this idea is not sacred. I want to hear your criticism of it. It may be a really bad idea or maybe it's one you can improve upon. Just don't be afraid to give me your opinion, because if you don't give me an opinion, you're not very useful to me. If you always agree with me, you're not very useful. So I'm giving you permission to challenge this idea.' Leaders need to give people an opportunity and permission to challenge.

"The other thing you can do to make good followers," added Rich, "is to tell them it's okay to fail. You can say, 'Look, I expect you to take some risks. I expect that you're going to fail sometimes. If you're not failing once in a while, you're not taking enough risks. There is no punishment for failure. In fact, the reward is that you learn a lot from failure.' You've got to create a safe environment for followers so that they can really offer everything they have without fear, guilt, worry about failure, or concern for contradicting the leader."

Empowerment. People need leaders to turn them loose without fear of reprisal. That gave me an idea for the next topic to discuss, after I returned from another main-stage transition.

CHAPTER 12

TEAM BUILDING

AFTER OUR CONVERSATION ABOUT helping people to become better followers, it seemed only reasonable to talk about what it takes to develop leaders into better teams. As had been brought up in an earlier discussion, no leader has all the gifts and skills necessary to provide all the leadership competencies required to succeed. The best way to maximize one's talents and to ensure success is to work as part of a team of leaders.

I'd had the privilege of spending a few years studying leadership teams and had written a book about what I discovered. The lessons were so powerful that ever since that experience I have always advocated the use of teams. Whenever I find an organization that is beholden to a single leader, my chief recommendation is that they rescue both that leader and the organization by teaming him or her with other leaders who have complementary leadership aptitudes. But I was eager to hear what our experts would say about the role of teams among leaders.

As expected, the feeling was unanimous that teams are a superior approach to solo leadership. A team always outperforms an individual; it's a simple mathematical principle. And our experts were pretty consistent in their views about how teams of leaders work best.

Ken Blanchard has been around the block a few times and seen more than his fair share of leaders and leadership teams. He opened our interaction by unequivocally stating the value of a team approach.

"If you have an area that you're weak on, hire people who cover your weakness. That's a really powerful way to do it. None of us is as smart as all of us. One of my favorite recent books is *Team of Rivals*. It's about Abraham Lincoln when he ran for president. The guys who ran against him were all more experienced, and they hated each other and Lincoln. And when he finally won the election, Lincoln went to each one of those rivals and said, 'I need you because you have this strength and this capacity.' All of them turned out to admire him. They all called him magnanimous. He had this belief that it's amazing how much you can get done if you don't care who gets the credit."

Laurie Beth Jones concurred with Ken's view and suggested that the way to develop those kinds of leadership teams is to take account of your strengths and join with people whose strengths are your weaknesses. "I agree with Buckingham and his research at Gallup that the most important thing is to identify your strengths. That's the way God made you. He doesn't want a tiger to act like an ox. And it's really not effective or even pretty to watch one try to become the other. So the important thing is to understand how you are wired and what you came here to do, and then realize that you do not have the whole picture; then you can surround yourself with people who are complementary to you and who know how to fill in the gaps. It's harmful when leaders do not see the strengths that others can bring because they think they have it all. Those are dangerous people."

While he generally agreed with Ken and Laurie Beth, Patrick Lencioni raised a caution about using the identification of your weaknesses as an excuse not to keep growing.

"I'm not a believer in only focusing on your strengths, because I think there's a humility in understanding what you are not good at. Yes, God gave you strengths and you should use them. But the reason you have to know your weaknesses is that some of those are the things that keep you from being a good leader or a better person." He acknowledged that he was not calling for people to ignore their limitations. "Surround yourself with people who don't have your weaknesses. I am aware of my weaknesses and unafraid to call them out. It's just practical sense to supplement my strengths with other people's different strengths. But beyond that, some of the things I'm not good at, I should get better at."

It seemed that the disagreement had to do with matters of balance: how much time should be invested in shoring up weaknesses rather than exercising strengths. But there was no disagreement about the importance of teaming leaders whose strengths made the aggregate more capable.

Patrick offered other advice from his extensive experience in how teams work. "Teams should be smaller rather than larger. When you have more than eight people, the team breaks down. Chris Argyris of Harvard told us years ago that in order to communicate effectively, you have to have two kinds of communication: advocacy and inquiry. When you get more than seven or eight people at a meeting, they stop inquiring and it's more likely you'll just have people advocating a certain position.

"And every team needs a leader, even if it's a team made up of leaders. There needs to be someone who is the ultimate tiebreaker, but if that person is doing a good job, he or she rarely has to exercise that authority. I'm not a believer in self-managed teams. When I work on teams where nobody is in charge—we are all equal—that's a recipe for the freeloader effect, where people can claim it wasn't their job."

Patrick was describing what teams often call their captain—the person who is generally on equal footing with the rest of the group but must occasionally step in to settle decisions or make sure that the team stays on task. Ralph Winter, who builds multiple teams every time he produces a movie, gave us some helpful guidance on the process of getting a team to be functional.

"Part of building an effective team is getting everyone on the same page or heading in the same direction, toward the same goal. That enables us to get some agreement about what kind of product we are creating and why. In my case, getting everyone on the same page means that we have a common understanding of what kind of movie we are making, why we are making it, and who we are making it for. This has to happen before we get on the set. On every project I work on, there are a number of other producers, rights holders, and, of course, the studio, so it's a bit like herding cats. We go through a litany of discussions about what we're trying to accomplish and how we will do that. Invariably there are lots of different agendas that everybody brings to the process, and building a successful team is trying to thread the needle. The producer has his agenda. The studio has its agenda. My fellow producing partner has her agenda. We need everybody to be heading in the same direction. People's expectations grow if you don't talk to them and make those connection points. Effective teams require constant communication on every issue on every project."

Ralph's emphasis on communication brought Ken back into the conversation. "I'll give you a good example of that. Look at Ronald Reagan. He had that capacity to gather people around him and listen. And I think God wants us to listen more than speak. Otherwise He would have given us two mouths."

"I tend to be a participative leader," agreed Rich Stearns. His experience with numerous leadership teams had led him to extol the virtues of listening more than speaking. "I try to get good discussions going and listen a lot. I don't tell people what the answer is. I try to uncover or discover the answer through dialogue and by stimulating conversation. I like to get strong people assembled in a team and recognize that the team has a lot more ability to discover answers than any individual. If you can unleash the potential of a team of very strong people who have different opinions and backgrounds, you can come up with better answers than if you make the decisions in silos without that kind of group interaction."

Patrick was insistent, though, that the dialogue that takes place within a team be frank and open. "I'm looking for honest differences of opinion and maybe even a little bit of discomfort. One of the things I have recently come to conclude is that one of the biggest problems we face in our organizations is the fear of discomfort or having uncomfortable moments. I was with a group of CEOs the other day, and they hate having to call somebody on something or disagree with somebody. They will do anything to avoid emotion. People ask me to tell them good stories about people fighting in meetings. The truth of the matter is that most leaders go out of their way to avoid it.

"I like to see passion and even some emotion in meetings," he continued. "When I go to a meeting and nobody seems invested—you know, they're sharing information and data but not real opinions, and there's very little angst—I think that they can't possibly be performing as a team. Think about it. If you hung out with a married couple for a week and there was never a disagreement about anything, and I don't mean they had to be at each other's throats, but if they never disagreed, you might not hold out much hope for that marriage, because they're not helping to make the other person a better version of him- or herself. I don't like it when my wife tries to make me a better version of myself, but I love her for making me better. Teams must be the same way."

"And if you allow a team to get bogged down with noncontributors, then you are basically dead," added Jimmy Blanchard. "I mean, if you're carrying noncontributors on your leadership teams, you are dead as a high-performance growth company." He underscored the importance of Ralph's comments. "And that is always a question of constantly communicating, constantly clarifying values and culture, and constantly recasting and improving strategy in coming up with plans.

"Probably more than anything else, though, teams succeed by constantly admonishing and encouraging each other. The most important thing to build in a team is openness, where you invite discussion and heed conflict. If you are having meetings and everybody feels uncomfortable with a decision but just says, 'Okay, boss, that's right, whatever you say,' you ain't got much of a team. You've got to be able to thrash it out and roll up your sleeves and argue with each other and tell the boss he is crazy. And when the team is done meeting, everybody has to walk out and get along and be on the same page."

I was reminded of some of the organizations I had observed while studying team dynamics. At first, before I understood the process, I was horrified at how some teams would get behind closed doors and rumble. I mean they just went at it, no holds barred, yelling and cajoling and arguing with each other. It took me a while to recognize three important things that were happening. First, they were testing and improving the ideas they would eventually embrace. By probing every nook and cranny of everything on the table, they made sure that they would be pursuing the best they had to offer. Second, each leader had a chance to get a hearing of his or her views. Third, they were developing their trust in each other, allowing each person's strengths to emerge in their common desire to do and be the best possible. Behind those closed doors, everything was up for grabs, nothing was sacred, and everyone had an equal chance to mix it up. But once those doors opened, the team was unified and tight, watching out for each other and cohesive in their approach. Having worked in several highly dysfunctional teams, watching this process was a marvel. And so were the results that such teams produced.

The most important thing to build in a team is openness, where you invite discussion and heed conflict.

But I also knew that building such teams is no simple task, and bringing together good leaders into a team environment does not automatically produce a viable team. John Townsend spoke about his observations of leadership teams, noting that certain components need to be present in healthy teams.

"First of all, it takes spending time together. You can talk about teams all day, but unless you intentionally structure formal and informal settings in which team members can interact, it's just another good idea. Carving out time from other things so these leaders can get together and find out they enjoy the energy and interchange and stimulation and personalities—that's crucial.

"And then you have to show people the results of that dynamic—show them that they are much more effective in reaching their goals and investing their gifts in the furtherance of the mission when they are in teams. In other words, they need to see that it is not only enjoyable working together as a team, but that everybody is bearing fruit too."

A common question people had asked me over the years was whether leadership teams should be created by intentional design or if an organization should allow such teams to emerge organically. My own studies had shown that it is best when the teams are purposefully orchestrated. I had discovered that when you find a group of leaders whose skills complement those of the other team members—that is, a visionary, motivational leader; plus a strategic leader; plus a networking, mobilizing leader; plus an operational, systems-building leader—then you have the makings of something special. Chemistry is much less important than complementary skills if the individuals passionately share the same vision.

John had come to the same conclusion. "Bringing together the people on the team must be intentional, because by nature people either isolate or they have their own club with the people they feel the safest with. And one thing a leader does is get people out of their comfort zones to do what is not natural, which is to say, 'I will give up individual preferences for the greater good.' Sometimes you have to herd the cattle the way the cattle didn't want to go in the first place."

That assessment was further supported by Colleen Barrett. Southwest has long promoted the idea of leadership teams. "You have got a real team if everybody is working for the same cause and knows what his or her contribution is that will lead to ultimate success. In other words, everyone matters. You honor and respect everybody's contributions. You listen, you learn, and you lead together."

My mind wandered back to the research I'd read about failed businesses and how most of them had suffered from solo leadership systems. My own research had shown a substantial difference in performance between organizations that relied on leadership teams and those that did not. And now the experts assembled at the conference were united in their belief that teams are the only way to go. It seemed clear that using teams of leaders working together toward a shared vision is a no-brainer. Anything less would be cheating the organization and its constituency out of the best that it has to offer.

CHAPTER 13

FAITH AND
MORALS

AS I LOOKED AROUND the greenroom and thought for a minute about the background of these world-class leaders, I was struck by the fact that so many of them had either referenced a belief and trust in a higher power or at least indicated that effective leaders need a source of moral authority beyond themselves. With faith playing such a significant role in recent presidential elections, in business ethics discussions, and other recent world events, it seemed like a reasonable subject to research more thoroughly and directly with these people.

Upon my mentioning the matter to a small group of leaders, Bob Dees was the first to respond.

"Napoleon once said the moral is to the physical as three is to one. He recognized that physical things on the battlefield are important but that moral, spiritual, and emotional things are even more important. He recognized that a little piece of ribbon pinned on a soldier's uniform is far more powerful than years of training. Simple recognition of one's efforts is a powerful tool. We spend a lot of time teaching soldiers how to fire their weapons. That's skill. But even more important is their will. Why do they fire it, when do they fire it, can they fire it in the face of daunting odds or opposing fire?"

The thread of Bob's statement drew John Kotter into the conversation as he reflected on the role of moral authority in leading people. "Power is inherently a part of management and leadership. The issue there is using it with intelligence and respect for others, with some sense of moral direction. There's no question that you need people at the top of organizations who help provide some sort of moral framework, which is what leaders naturally do. Think of all the great leaders throughout history, the ones we really do think of as great. They all provided a moral framework. That goes beyond the politics or the product or the finances, and it's part of why they succeeded. Moral authority is a very powerful piece of what the really great leaders have. So many of the great leaders of our time do not derive their power from position; they derive it from a certain moral authority. The Martin Luther King Jrs. of the world are big examples of that."

I wondered aloud if, in our increasingly secular and pluralistic society, leaders these days would even know what *moral authority* means. Sure, they might be accorded such authority by the people they lead, but what is it based upon? With business schools dropping their business ethics classes because even the faculty cannot agree on what should be taught in such a class, is there much reason to believe that leaders will continue to operate with moral authority rather than simply exercise raw power based on amoral personal choices and preferences?

"Leaders operate with kind of a generic moral philosophy of what life is all about," John explained. "It's related to a three-word saying that is connected to choices in a number of different ways. The three words are *all God's children*. And one way they get connected to leadership is that leaders think that we all have the responsibility for taking care of all God's children. That may sound like a bit much for a businessman, and maybe it is, with the extreme way that I've said it in that sentence, but there is that breadth of outlook and responsibility that tends to be inherent in good leaders all the time."

That concept was tied into the role of faith in leadership by Barry Black.

"Faith and morality ultimately affect how you lead because they affect you. I love the statement Paul makes in Acts 24:16. He says, "I myself always strive to have a conscience without offense toward God and men" [NKJV]. I think that talks about a spirituality where you can live in such a way that you're transparent. I call it the Daniel test. When Daniel's enemies were trying to trap him with his prayer life, they sent people to follow him around, and they ended up actually giving him a tribute. They said they could not find anything against Daniel except that he followed the laws of his God.

"Now, if someone were surreptitiously following a leader, what would be unearthed? So your spirituality is a part of your moral authority, and once you lose your moral authority you've lost your ability to lead. We see many examples of great leaders who were discovered in unethical activity, and they lost a critical part of their ability to lead. Aristotle, in his book on rhetoric, refers to it as *ethos*, and he's talking about an individual who is ethically congruent, whose rhetoric is backed by his or her actions. And that is why your spirituality is critically important: it ultimately affects the person you are. It's the old Lincoln thing: you can't fool all the people all of the time. Your spirituality becomes very important."

But where does that moral authority come from? Is it awarded by the people? Is it delivered by God? Does a leader just assume it? Is it positional? How does that work in practice? There was some debate internally about that. One perspective was offered by Jon Gordon.

"Moral authority is moving the organization toward that bigger purpose to accomplish something meaningful, something socially responsible, to have an impact on the greater good. And when you have moral authority and use it in that way, trust is built because you are walking the walk. You get that authority simply by saying what you are going to do and doing what you say.

"Moral authority is a matter of integrity and trust," Jon added, thinking about what he had witnessed in his consulting efforts. "You build that trust by being engaged in the process with people: by caring about them, by serving in the trenches with them, by being visible, by expressing appreciation, by asking questions and listening to their opinions.

Moral authority is moving the organization toward that bigger purpose to accomplish something meaningful, something socially responsible, to have an impact on the greater good.

"That kind of leader has moral authority. And he or she retains it by creating a culture that values people and employees and takes care of them and the customer. As a leader, you have to model that thinking and that behavior. Moral authority is achieved by walking the walk of integrity, by doing what is in the best interest of the team, and by truly caring about others and the organization."

The notion of earning and maintaining moral authority struck a chord with Mike Huckabee. His years of service in ministry and government had afforded him the time to study and think about the source of moral authority, as well as an insider's view—and personal experience—regarding its use.

"People sometimes say you have to make decisions that violate your morals. I say, quite honestly, no, you don't. When I was governor, I made decisions that were politically hurtful, or not clearly understood by people, but I didn't feel compelled to lie or cheat or do something that was basically dishonest in order to get what I wanted. I never thought of doing that.

"One of the big challenges for many Christians who get involved in political issues is they want to transfer the purity of theology into political practice. Theology is pure; heaven, hell, light, dark, the devil. It's easy to be real black-and-white with theology. But politics is the art of doable, so if we want to lead a pro-life cause, well, how pro-life is it? If we advance the ball and get some restrictions on the practice of abortion, that's what's doable for right now. I would like to see all human life protected. We can't do that right now, but we can help the ball move down the field and have the Fetal Protection Act and informed consent. If we get that far, should I say that we failed to protect human life? We succeeded in getting done what we could get done. Sometimes the legislation won't be just like we want it to be, but if we have advanced and haven't given up, that's the part we have to accept."

Mike had raised an interesting perspective: the exercise of moral authority is not always an all-or-nothing proposition. But moral authority, going back to Jon's concept, is also about not giving up when you are pursuing what you believe to be morally right. Like everything else in life, getting to those outcomes is a process that takes time and energy but also consistency and diligence.

Jon returned to the dialogue with some thoughts about the source of such authority and the way faith influences one's ability to lead. "A lot of people aren't spiritual, or aren't Christian, and when you describe the role of faith in establishing moral authority and even in developing a positive attitude in the face of difficult times and challenges, they look at you like they're thinking, *Faith? What's that? Come on, tell me something more. That can't be the answer!* I understand that because I really evolved with this in my own life." Jon described how he had been raised in a Jewish family and had eventually come to accept Jesus Christ as the Messiah and his Savior. From our prior conversations, I knew what a dramatic impact that conversion has had on Jon's life.

"I used to think a lot more about your own positive energy, your own positive thinking, but now I have come to believe it's more about truly relying on your faith and on God more than yourself. You can have conviction and believe in yourself as a leader, but you have to have an even greater faith in God. In fact, my favorite verse in the Bible is, 'I can do all things through Christ who strengthens me.'"

That line of thought moved us into a discussion about the role of faith in leadership. Because I have argued that a leader is someone with three qualities—God's calling to lead, character that pleases God and allows Him to entrust the leader with authority, and the core competencies to get things done that fulfill a God-given vision—I raised the matter of calling, and whether a Christian leader has a different kind of calling than a leader who is not a follower of Christ.

Mike Huckabee, who is highly regarded by people across the faith spectrum, even though he has been very transparent and open about his personal commitment to Christ, expressed the opinion that Christians who lead probably do have a different calling. "A leader who is a Christian has to be concerned about not just his own reputation, but also the Lord's. For instance, you would not want to treat people in such a way that their view of Jesus is their view of you and it's not a good one. You have a responsibility to be a reflection of who He is. Some of that is about follow-up and taking the time to explain your decisions. If, for example, you have to take somebody out of a position, it's not a matter of just throwing him or her out of the bus."

Christians in a leadership position do, indeed, have a different calling according to Laurie Beth Jones. She explained that is because of the identity of the higher authority to whom Christians are responsible. "Everyone has to have a higher authority. When you get a CEO who believes his authority comes from the board, which is comprised of shareholders or people who represent shareholders, then that CEO is going to answer to that board. It can initiate a cycle of ineptitude and mediocrity if you have a board of people who are only looking out for the dollar, because that is going to drive their decisions. The CEO is under their authority, and he or she can be doing the right things but failing to meet their demand for a financial return of certain proportions. We have seen this played out in the nation's financial collapse. If a leader is instead looking to do what Jesus would do, and to discern how God sees the situation, then it gives him or her a whole different perspective."

It seemed that we were touching on moral authority and faith as the source of the values that are promoted and executed by leaders. Like Jon Gordon, Michael Franzese had gone through an extraordinary transformation in faith and morals. He understood the transition in values firsthand.

"When Christ was not in my life and I was in a criminal lifestyle, I had developed the ability to justify certain things in my life that were just not right. Your life becomes very Machiavellian, where the ends justify the means. For instance, in my former life, government agencies were always a target. I didn't respect the government, because I always felt that it was the enemy. So defrauding the government out of taxes was technically a crime, but morally it wouldn't have been a crime to me because I saw them as the bad guys and myself as the good guy. That's how I thought at that point in time; I was able to justify wrong things as morally correct. Once Christ came in my life, I realized that that was a mistaken way of thinking and a mistaken way of leading others. Obviously I'd led people in the wrong direction. Now, with Christ in my life, I lead people differently, and I would not lead anybody down that path."

A leader who is a Christian has to be concerned about not just his own reputation, but also the Lord's.

Newt Gingrich built on that foundation regarding the basis of decision making. "Without a sense of your faith, how do I know how you'll make decisions? There's a difference between my judging whether you belong to the right faith and my knowing whether or not you take life seriously. Do you believe that life has more than an immediate, existential, hedonistic meaning? Do you believe that you are the inheritor of a long tradition of human beings striving for good, and that you are in the end going to shape the world of your children and grandchildren and that you have a moral obligation in that?

"I think that part of what broke the Republicans in Congress in 2006," Newt continued, moving from the philosophic to the pragmatic, "is that they forgot that power without meaning is nihilism, and nihilism allows you to become corrupted, because you have no barriers against it. In a very real sense, the law, in the Anglo-Saxon, American tradition, is what binds us to block evil. All of us are capable of falling to temptation, all of us will fall short and will do things that are wrong, and we need to be bounded by civilization. So we have to ask someone who wants to be a real leader if he or she gets that."

Ralph Winter took Newt's thoughts further down the road of practical application. "Hopefully your faith affects how you deal with people in that you have a sensitivity, a respect level, and a worldview that underpins the way you deal with them. You have to pay people a fair wage and be truthful about that. When you fire them, you have to tell them the truth and not sugarcoat it. You have to follow the law.

"I'm going to do all of those things that I'm required to do, but try to do it with a sense of humanity. I try to fire people so they will say thank you. That's happened a few times. Even letting people go, helping them understand why it happened, letting them know it's not because they were bad people but because they failed to meet the objectives—and as people, they still have value. They will find another job. There's a way to let someone go without being a jerk, and our faith should inform the way we go about doing that and the way we can be more human in that process. Leaders don't have to do their job in a dehumanizing way."

Ralph and others had alluded to the fact that as they retooled themselves as leaders, their faith had become a source of strength. As I thought about all the difficult and harsh tasks that a good leader must do, I had to wonder what compels and energizes someone to push through the challenging times. Faith seemed to be one of the sources of strength, if not the central source, for the journey.

During Ken Melrose's years at Toro, he'd been in various positions and had faced all kinds of hardships, including overseeing the company when it was on the verge of bankruptcy. He talked a bit about what a difference his faith in Christ meant to him as a leader during those times of trial. "There were times when I thought, *I'm not up to this.* When Toro was about to go bankrupt and people were leaving the company and the CEO was about to leave the company, the board called me on a Saturday morning. I was painting the living room of my house, and the chairman of the board called me up and asked if I'd come over and meet with him. I didn't even know who he was at first because the chairman of the board didn't usually call me on the phone. In fact, he had never called me, so I didn't recognize his voice. I think he was a little put out when he said, 'This is David' and I said, 'David who?' and here he was, the chairman of the board.

"So I went over to his house, and he had some other board members there. He said, 'We'd like you to become the head of the company and bail us out of this problem. The company is losing a lot of money.' Toro had all kinds of issues and it looked like we might not survive. I heard his request, and I was thinking to myself, *Who, me? Why me? I'm not prepared for this.* The task that lay ahead just to keep us afloat was monumental, and they wanted me to be in charge of leading the recovery and ensuring that we'd survive. I just didn't know if I was up to that. I was a marketing person, a grower. One of the first tasks after I took the position was going to be terminating over half of our employees and closing most of our plants. The idea of standing up in front of all the employees in a plant and telling them that we were going to close the plant and they didn't have jobs anymore— well, I just felt I couldn't do it. I knew I needed help.

"So I got a sign, framed it, and put it up in my office. I knew that God would not let me do things beyond my own limitations, that He would be there to help me. I figured that somehow this was what God wanted me to do, even though I wasn't so sure that I wanted to do it. So I put up a sign that said, God meant for you to be here . . . now! It was a very visible sign, framed and all, and I put it on the wall opposite my desk so when I'd come in the office, I'd see that sign, first thing. If I was on the phone and I was looking over at this wall, or if I had some people in my office around the table, I could see it.

"Those were critical times, and I had some doubts about myself and talked to myself about the situation. *Am I up to this? Well, I'm not, but God and I are. As long as God's with me, I'm going to be okay, because I'm not doing this alone.* And that sign was kind of a beacon for me; it gave me the encouragement to convince myself, *Aw, I can do this. It's going to be messy and terrible, and I'm going to hate parts of it, but it's the right thing to do. It's a calling, and it's what I believe God wants me to do now.* So as I led the company, I gained the confidence to tell people that I had some philosophies about servant leadership and empowerment and creating trust in the organization. I reminded them that we didn't have much to lose because we might otherwise go bankrupt and go away. But we didn't go bankrupt, because I led them to believe we were going to survive, and we were going to survive this way and with God's help."

There were smiles all around the group. Even some of the leaders present who were probably not devout followers of any faith were intrigued by the power that Ken had drawn from his conviction that he was called to take that unappealing position, and his certainty that with the help of God he would be able to do some special things at a hurting company. His strength had come from his faith in God and from constant reminders, such as that sign, that God does not give us more than we can handle if we commit to doing the right thing according to His principles. And there is nothing about His principles that conflicts with good business practice.

By this time Lou Taylor was all fired up too. She gave us her point of view about the importance of faith as a source of strength and guidance, even in the very secular and hard-nosed world of entertainment in which she was immersed.

"The spiritual faith of a leader, that's everything. And I don't think you can give away what you don't possess. There was a real difficult revelation for me. In the book of Joshua you read about when Joshua had entered into the Promised Land and he chose not to seek the Lord when the whole mess with the Gibeonites happened. Of course that became an issue for him, and from that point on Joshua ceased to hear the voice of the Lord again until he started to obey God. Something that struck me in those chapters is that Joshua was the man who was responsible for communing with the Lord; he took the instructions that the Lord gave him and then he executed them.

That caused me to look at him for the first time ever as a pastor, realizing that he was shepherding the children of Israel at the same time that he also had a job, because he was the commander of the army.

"What a revelation that was for me, personally," confided Lou as she relived that time of discovery. "There was Joshua, in the trenches with these people, doing his job as a commander of an army, but he also had the responsibilities of a pastor—he was that connection, so to speak, to the Lord. So if I don't have that connection to the Lord and I'm not hearing from Him and I'm not following instructions and I'm not being guided in the Spirit, then what can I pass on to my staff as far as the vision goes? How can I lead my clients forward?

"When I'm in my office," she firmly stated, "I am the commander of the army in that office. I'm in the trenches, dealing with the dark side of fame, celebrity, money, sex, and all the rest. But I also have to serve as a shepherdess to the people who work here. How am I ever going to give anybody hope if I'm not connected to the Lord, but at the same time carry out my job as an absolute battle maiden for my clients?"

Lou had done a great job of capturing the challenge of having a foot in two worlds: the world of fulfilling one's responsibilities in the marketplace and the world of integrating one's faith principles into every dimension of life. Leaders who operate from a base of faith face that challenge every day. But Wilson Goode placed it in a good perspective.

"I have always believed that if I trust in God, He will see me through. I cannot remember a day in public office when I had any doubt or any fear that God would abandon me. I cannot recall waking up in the morning and saying, 'I wonder if everything around me is going to fall apart.' I woke up every morning in anticipation that no matter what the problem was, at the end of the turmoil and all of the stuff that was going on, God was going to set me on a high mountain, and I was going to come out on top."

The heartfelt recollections from Lou and Wilson drew my thoughts back to a favorite passage of scripture, Proverbs 3:5-6, where Solomon writes: "Trust in the LORD with all your heart; do not depend on your own understanding. Seek his will in all you do, and he will show you which path to take" (NLT).

Not every leader will motivate, mobilize, resource, and direct people toward a vision on the strength of their belief that God is with them, guiding their thoughts and actions. But I couldn't help but believe that those who do will find the going smoother, the challenges less overwhelming, and the improbable results more likely to achieve.

CHAPTER 14

POWER

I RETURNED TO THE GREENROOM after introducing Warren Bennis to the audience. For more than four decades, Warren has been teaching and speaking about leadership. I headed straight for the vacant couch at the far end of the room and plopped down, hoping to listen to Warren's presentation on the wise use of power in effective leadership.

He had already begun his talk, but I was able to watch and listen as he was making some early points.

"When I was in the army I began to see that there were some leaders in the infantry, on the front lines, who seemed to avoid casualties more than others," Warren recalled, slowly pacing from side to side on the stage. "There were some leaders who seemed to have more men sent back because of trench fighting or frostbite, and it seemed they weren't taking care of their men. That not only intrigued me, but because we were playing for mortal stakes, I wanted to know what was really going on there. Why were there differences?

"When I began studying with my major mentor, Captain Gardener, he made it very clear to me that there are several kinds of power. He said, 'You know, Warren, influence is a result of power.' Influence, to use graduate school language, is the dependent variable. But power is the source of that which leads to behavior.

"Now, in most organizations power is defined coercively. I have power because I control the means to your satisfaction. I can tell you when you're going on vacation or not. I can handle your promotions and if you're going to make one or not. I control your pay, your working hours, the number of classes you're going to teach. That's power, and it's really coercive. It doesn't mean we don't use it. Most bureaucracies work like that. It's neither bad nor good; it's just the way things are, and it can be bad or good based on the relationship.

"So then think about the power that comes from the relationship, the power of a person identifying with a leader and adopting his goals and feeling inspired. We identify with leaders and their ideas. We identify with their goals. You see, that's another form of power. And another form of power is group power, which we call reference power. It, too, is coercive.

Influence is a result of power.

"Yet another type is expert power. Go to a lawyer, go to a doctor, and if you're thinking again about influence as a result of power, then the doctor, the judge, the lawyer, the engineer—whoever the expert may be, you don't always have to take his or her point of view, but in most cases you're going to listen very closely.

"Still another type is network power or access power. For example, I know that I have power at the university because I am able to help students get into graduate school, or I can help our PhD candidates get jobs. I can help colleagues get published, because I can open doors."

Warren was on a roll, and it was a good roll at that. While he was speaking, my friend Michael Franzese had come over to sit next to me on the couch. As both of us are from New York and have remained die-hard Yankees fans over the years, we enjoy ribbing each other about our roots. As Warren surged forward, I turned to Michael and asked if he'd been following Warren's presentation. He nodded his head in the affirmative. Knowing that Michael had done a lot of thinking over the years about the nature and the use of power, I asked him what he thought of what he'd heard so far.

"Listen, this guy is brilliant," Michael said respectfully. For the next few moments we listened to Warren's words.

"And if you have a Machiavellian view of human nature, you're going to operate out of fear, definitely; out of respect, perhaps when you're at your best; but out of a desire to manipulate, always."

I figured that statement would hit one of Michael's hot buttons—and it did. Perhaps reflecting on his own book on leadership contrasts between the Machiavellian and Judeo-Christian approaches to leadership, Warren had stimulated Michael's thoughts with his comments.

"You know, George," Michael said as he repositioned himself on the couch, looking directly at me, "the hunger for power is a horrible thing. In the life that I led, that search for power always led to destruction. Always. I have never seen a power-hungry person survive; it eventually catches up to you. You can't survive it. Power is such a dangerous thing if it's not used properly. You should always lead with the recognition that you have power, but without making power the central reason for which you lead."

Before I could respond to Michael's words of wisdom, Newt Gingrich, who had come up behind us and was following the conversation, offered his rejoinder to Michael.

"Power is very dangerous," he reaffirmed. "The greatest danger of power is that it gets you to believe that you are not really mortal—and, of course, you are. It's an inherent problem of power. The Roman ruler once told the general during a triumphal parade, 'Remember, you are only a man.' That's why democracies and the rule of law are so central to the human experience. In the absence of the rule of law and the absence of people having the right to fire you, the leader inevitably begins to believe his own PR and begins to write ever more grotesque PR."

I decided to go with the flow and see where this trail would take us. And there was no telling where that destination might be, because now we had attracted a half dozen other leaders around the couch. I felt like the pied piper of leadership that day—and was honored to be included in that company of people.

Why, I asked the new formation of leaders, was power such a problem? We're all big boys and girls, we know right from wrong, we have the internal capacity to wield power wisely. Why don't we? What's the big deal? Are we so beholden to our emotions and egos that we just cannot help ourselves, so we allow our weaknesses and dark sides to reign?

Jimmy Blanchard jumped all over that one, as if it were a home run ball served up in a slow-pitch softball game. "George, I became the CEO of our company at a very young age; I was just twenty-nine. So I came in not knowing a lot about where I was going or what I wanted to do. I basically was a quiet leader at first, and initially I wasn't on a path to reach a specific vision or target. Thankfully, I gravitated into what we now call servant leadership."

This whole concept of servant leadership was something that was first proposed in the 1980s by Robert Greenleaf, in his seminal book by that name. A number of leaders have since promoted that approach to leadership, including Ken Blanchard, who was also in our midst by this time.

"Of course, we didn't call it servant leadership. I mean, nobody had ever heard of that term until the Greenleaf book made it very popular, and much later Ken Blanchard came along with the Lead Like Jesus movement. I only wish today, at age sixty-seven, that I had known what I know now back at age twenty-nine."

Jimmy was interrupted by someone in our contingent who asked him exactly what servant leadership was all about.

"Servant leadership is all about modeling the life of Jesus as the perfect example of serving others in the midst of providing them with leadership. True servant leadership is all about getting a handle on our own selfishness."

It turned out that we not only had a bunch of devoted servant leaders around the couch, but many of them were also vocal advocates for that approach to leading. One of them, Mike Huckabee, continued where Jimmy had left off.

"The servant leader model—which I think is a biblically correct model for any realm in which you lead, whether it's corporate, political, or otherwise—is a transformative model, because you are not trying to build loyalty so that people will improve your position. You commit your loyalty to those around you, and the result of that is that they will elevate you to a higher level than you could ever elevate yourself to reach. Leadership is about empowering others around you and helping them to succeed. Then they will return and give you a level of success you could have never achieved on your own. But it will be a natural relationship rather than one in which you have to constantly tell them you are the leader."

Then Barry Black added more flesh to the bones of the servant leader apologetic. "The sine qua non of leadership is service," he started. I have to admit, having avoided Latin like the bubonic plague, I had no idea what he was talking about. I looked it up later and found out he meant that the essence of, or indispensable condition of leadership is serving others. "Jesus said in Matthew 20, 'I come not to be served, but to serve.' The apostle Paul said in 1 Corinthians 4:1, 'Consider us, as servants of Christ and stewards of the mysteries of God.' It does not mean that some of the other factors that you articulated will not play a part in the leadership dynamic, but service must always be the dominant motif of a leader."

True servant leadership is all about getting a handle on our own selfishness.

Now he was talking some stuff that I not only understood but also wholeheartedly agreed with. "Jesus said to His disciples, 'The kings of the Gentiles exercise lordship, but that's not the way it should be among you.' I think that

He was capturing His philosophy of leadership. And I think that one of the reasons why the old saw 'People don't care how much you know until they know how much you care' is so true for effective leadership is that when you serve, you do care and you demonstrate that you care. When you look at how Jesus led, you just see this tremendous improvement in the service of those around Him from the time He left heaven until the time He ascended. It was all about serving. For me, service is the dominant theme of leadership."

Those thoughts received a hearty endorsement from Bob Dees, who revealed that he had not entered the military as a servant leader. "One of the biggest changes in my views on leadership relates to the notion of serving. Effective leaders in any sector have got to be servant leaders. In *Good to Great*, Jim Collins writes that the two criteria of truly effective, great leaders are passion and humility. But how are those developed?"

We waited for a second while Bob gathered his thoughts and answered his own question. "When I was a cadet at West Point I was taught that you need to take care of your troops. Later, when I went through infantry officer training, again they drove home the point that you have to take care of the troops. So I knew that requirement and gave mental assent to the fact that I ought to take care of the troops.

"As a young officer I took care of the troops, but I did it because I knew I was supposed to take care of the troops. Somewhere along the way, though, I transitioned from taking care of the troops to loving the troops. It went from my head to my heart. I don't know when that happened; maybe it was the first time I saw a soldier give his life for another one; or maybe it was when I had to gather Easter eggs with a young widow and her child because her husband had hidden those eggs on the eve of Easter, then committed suicide; or maybe it was in a combat setting. And then it transitioned again and went from a passion within my heart to a divine calling. It took on a sense of the spiritual, the noble, that this was God-inspired.

"That was a profound formulation for me, seeing that servant leadership is the essence of Jesus Christ and the essence of what it means to be a Christian leader. That was later validated over time by books like *Good to Great*—servant leadership is the bedrock of effective leadership. I had learned models that instilled the idea in my head, but experientially it was done by watching somebody under my command die. There's an expression in the military: threat clears a man's head—when that happens, you're very teachable. As you go through the military and you see threats on your own life and on the lives of others, it clears your own head, and you grasp with crystal clarity the essence of some of these things."

As often happens when military leaders share from their experience, there was a new level of somberness as we absorbed the lesson Bob had imparted through the crucible of his wartime undertakings. There couldn't have been a better follow-up to that moment than the wisdom of another soft-spoken leader, Tony Dungy.

"The biggest thing that changed my perspective was when I heard a pastor talking about the Middle Eastern shepherd, and that was the example that Christ used so often, and why He is referred to as the Good Shepherd. I really didn't know what that meant until it was described to me, but the shepherd, in that part of world, was always in front of the sheep. The sheep always followed him, and the sheep could go anywhere, basically, and then upon the call of his voice, they would know which way they were supposed to go. It is totally different than our understanding of what we see in a cattle drive where the wranglers herd cattle.

"The more I thought about it and studied it," Tony told us, "the more clear it was that the shepherd takes care of the sheep so well that they come to recognize the voice and know his presence and what he wants them to do, and they follow because they think that is the best thing for them. They know they are being provided for. The shepherd knows the way to go and they follow. That has kind of shaped my style of leadership. The players and coaches that I have worked with know that I care about them enough to do everything that I can to get them to reach their goals. They are going to follow me because they want to, not because I have the position of leader and I'm the head coach and I make them do it. They do it because they believe that it is the best course in the long run."

Tony's discourse was helpful, because I had heard so many derogatory statements about the Bible referring to the followers of Christ simply as sheep—dumb animals who can't take care of themselves and are wholly dependent upon someone to give them hope. But Tony's insight into the historical role of shepherds was both enlightening and instructive. Sheep follow a shepherd because they come to realize that he cares enough about them to do what is best for them. Isn't that the kind of leader we all want to be: someone whom others can depend upon to look out for their best interests and deliver whatever they need to ensure their best outcomes? And as a sheep, that's certainly the kind of leader I'd want to produce for.

Another story in support of the servant leadership concept was then supplied by one of the most prolific advocates of this style, Ken Blanchard. "I was down in Texas with Southwest Airlines this summer. Gary Kelly was pointing out what the cost of gas is doing to their margins," Ken recounted, referring to the CEO of the airline. "Because they have such a clear vision, he said, 'There are two things we're not going to do. One is we're not going to raise the price of tickets significantly, because we're in the freedom business. We believe that every American should have the freedom to be with a friend or a relative in a happy time or a sad time, so why would we go against what we believe?'

"Then he mentioned the second thing they would not do, which was to do anything that would harm their people. Southwest thinks their most important resource is their people, even more than their customers, because if they don't motivate and inspire their people, they're not going to take care of their customers. Gary said, 'We're not going to get rid of people. We might cancel some flights, but we won't get rid of our people.' And what they did was to reach out to the whole organization to find out what suggestions everyone had for cutting costs. One of the recommendations they got, which they're seriously considering, was offered by one of the hourly people, who said, 'Let's eliminate uniforms. We've got thirty-four thousand people. We wouldn't have to buy the uniforms and we wouldn't have to clean them.' If you think about it, that's worth millions of dollars. But you see how they stuck to their values, and their behavior showed what it looks like to care about their people."

Bob saw the fit between Ken's story and his own experiences. "Leaders must choose to need their subordinates, and as they choose to need them and convey that attitude of empowerment and value and respect, a very powerful dynamic takes place."

Again, Bob had snuck in a simple thought that struck me as profound: leaders choosing to need those with whom they work. "Like so much in life, it's all about the choices we make. Perhaps we could even say that as leaders, we have chosen the outcomes we experience, whether those were the outcomes we desired or not. We choose the actual outcomes by virtue of how well we serve our fellow leaders and those who choose to follow us."

For a few minutes people shared some of their own war stories about how a servant mind-set in a leader changes the culture of the organization and empowers people to perform beyond expectations.

"Leaders need to know that their job and ultimate responsibility is to serve their people," Jon Gordon purposefully stated. "You serve them by investing in them: you develop them, encourage them, uplift them, inspire them. You don't do it just to be a good person—which, by the way, you become by doing that—but you also do it because it makes great business sense. The more you serve the people below you, and the more you empower and encourage them, the more likely they are to perform at a higher level and actually raise you and your organization to a higher level."

I gazed at the monitor and saw that Warren was wrapping up his session. Rats! I would have to get the DVD and listen to his entire presentation later—as I would with almost all of the sessions at the Master Leader Conference, since I'd been so engaged in these conversations. But why complain? Who else on the planet had experienced what I had during these two days? Fortunately DVDs of the big sessions were available, but the private sessions in the greenroom were a different matter. As I gathered myself to head back to the stage, thank Warren for his contribution, and then usher another great leader to the microphone, I focused on some closing words from Ken Melrose.

"Philosophically, leadership is about serving people. You want everyone to be productive and contributing for the organization to work, but if you have the decision-making power vested in just a few people who tell everyone else what to do, that's a leadership philosophy that simply will not get the best out of people. If everyone feels empowered, that they have accountability, and that they can make decisions and cannot be hurt by a bad decision, then you have a healthy process.

"The core of the philosophy is that we're all in this together. As the leader, my job is to make all these people work well together. There are times when a leader has to make a decision—maybe unilateral, sometimes autocratic—but that's out of a need in that instance, not representative of the core philosophy. A servant leadership or mentoring-coaching philosophy is not only sustainable but also makes the organization better all the time, because it enables people in the organization to make better decisions instead of relying on you alone to make all the decisions. It expands the power of the organization and enables performance goals to be met."

I felt pretty confident that if Warren had been in the room, he would have enjoyed the direction of that conversation.

CHAPTER 15

CRITICISM AND PRESSURE

IN MY HOTEL ROOM the night before, I had been pretty fried from the day's activity, so I had ordered room service and laid on the bed, watching a pair of movies. I'd seen them both before and loved each of them. One of them, *The American President*, features Michael Douglas as an incumbent president seeking reelection. The other was a small-budget film called *Facing the Giants*, about a football coach who leads his team from the dumps to the championship. Both films are heavy on leadership insights. But as I tossed and turned after the lights went out, my mind seemed to park on the manner in which the leaders in those stories handle criticism and pressure. In my own experience, those have been among the toughest challenges to master.

But hey, no problem. After all, I was at the Master Leader Conference. And I had a unique window into the minds of America's master leaders. I'd just ask them about these issues tomorrow.

Well, "tomorrow" was now, so after I returned to the greenroom I took advantage of one of my last chances to dig into this topic. I found a trio of heroes standing silently in front of a monitor off to the side, so I figured they were fair game for my next round of "Pick the Mind of the Leader." Actually, the three gentlemen arrayed near the screen were superb candidates for such a discussion: John Ashcroft, Lou Holtz, and Rich Stearns. Each of them had been through the fire. I was absolutely confident they would set me straight.

John was the first to volunteer a response regarding how he has handled pressure and criticism, especially in the aftermath of the September 11 atrocities. "I guess the thing that I might say here is that I kept my eyes on the prize. I didn't take my eyes off of what I wanted to do or get wrapped up in what people were saying. Since I left office I have found out about what some of the people were saying about me, and I look back and wonder if I would have been able to do what I needed to do if I had focused on people's reactions. People give me credit for being a much stronger person than I am.

"It's kind of interesting: a good friend of mine who is a very good leader from Missouri once told me, 'John, the dogs may bark, but the caravan moves on.' You have to understand what your objective is and not listen to the barking dogs. So how do you handle pressure? You keep your eyes on the prize. If it's noble, if it's the right thing, you just do it. For me, there's an element of trust in believing that things will somehow come out all right."

During my conversations with John I had found him to be a person who had truly been affected by the weight of the decisions he'd made while in public office. He took that responsibility seriously. But he also had a way of integrating his faith into his decision-making process, and once he was comfortable that he knew what the right thing to do actually was, he made the decision and kept moving forward. In that way, he was very similar to Lou Holtz—as Lou was about to point out.

"If you're going to be a leader, you're going to have adversity and you're going to have difficulty. You can count on it. My first year at South Carolina we inherited a very difficult situation. We went winless my first year. Now, we were 0 and 11, but records can be deceiving. We really weren't as good as our record would lead you to believe." We all cracked up at Lou's deadpan delivery and self-effacing commentary. "Everybody's criticizing you with nasty letters and on radio shows and in columns in the newspapers and magazines. But as a leader, you have to have a faith and a belief that you know where you're going to go and nothing in this world is going to keep you from getting there. In order to achieve success, you have to endure pain and sacrifice and overcome problems and obstacles.

"And is it hard? I should say so. That's why not many people are willing to be in a leadership role. The question you have to ask yourself is, *Am I willing to endure the difficulties in leadership in order to be successful, or am I going to give in to the negativity and the mediocrity that everybody comes to expect from losers?*

"I can't begin to tell you how many times after that 0 and 11 year I got down on my knees and prayed to God for the courage and the strength that when I walked in there, I could present an attitude that this is what we have to do. We don't like where we are, but the only thing that's going to change it from where we are today to where we'll be five years from now is the books we read, the people we meet, and the dreams we dream. We had some dreams, and we were going to continue to pursue them. And the minute they understood that I was as strong in my conviction in the times of adversity as I was when things were going well, that's when they responded to me.

"Was I discouraged? Was I downhearted? Absolutely. But I could not go into a meeting without praying that I would have the courage to show them the right attitude. You know what? It worked out. Twelve months later we had the second greatest turnaround in the history of NCAA football. We went from a winless season to number 17 in the country and beat Ohio State on January 1."

While Coach was speaking, I waved over a few other folks to join us. I could tell this would be another worthwhile adventure. When Lou finished, with a growing body of leaders now engaged, I asked him how he had managed to stay so focused on his goals. The pressure must have been incredible after an 0–11 season, especially given his high national profile as a coach.

Lou took it in stride and said, "Pressure is when you have to do something you aren't prepared to do. You have to understand what you want to do and what you're trying to do. I've never felt the pressure. Bear Bryant once said, 'Don't worry about making friends; don't worry about making enemies. Worry about winning, because if you win, your enemies can't hurt you, and if you lose, your friends can't stand you.' So you just try to go out and do the right thing and do it the best you can. You have a plan, you bring them in on that plan, and you believe that the plan will work.

"I really believed in our plan, even the first year in South Carolina when we were 0 and 11. You don't change plans; you work the plan. So we stuck with it, believed in it, and had a winning season; we were nationally ranked, and we won a big bowl game against Ohio State. You see, I believed in the plan, and even though it wasn't working at one time, that was because not everybody had bought into the plan and it was not implemented completely. So I always put more pressure on myself than anybody else did—the pressure of living up to my expectations. My expectations were higher than what other people had of me.

"And criticism—let me tell you, you can't worry about criticism. When you get criticized, you look at it and realize maybe it has some validity, maybe some of it is justified. If it is, then you need to change this or correct that. Or maybe you didn't know that was going on. Or maybe you realize the criticism is simply absurd. No matter what, you move on and you forget about it. You listen to it; you see if it's justified, and if it is then it will help you improve. Otherwise, you don't worry about it."

After noting that he wished Coach had been around to help some of Arkansas's teams, Mike Huckabee talked about the pressure and criticism he has faced in the political maelstrom. "In politics I had to learn to deal with the fact that life isn't fair. I had a hard time with that in the early days. I didn't mind criticism, because some of it was deserved, but I'm not interested in the manufactured, unfair, double-standard kind of criticism, because I have a sense of justice about me. When you make something up and beat me over the head with it and you haven't held others to the same standard, that's when my sense of justice kicks in and I want to say, 'Aw, come on. You are not only hitting me; you're kicking me, too. You didn't treat this with fairness.'

"But I learned that if I couldn't handle that, I'd better not play this game, because it is a full-contact sport. There'd be lots of blood, and some of it was going to be mine. So if I decided to play, I'd have to believe in myself and what I stood for, and I just had to expect I was going to come out of this thing okay.

"I tell you, when I ran for president I really had a much easier time than most people expected, because I went into it knowing it would be rough-and-tumble. It was, but to be honest with you, it wasn't as savage as other political races I've had. Running for president was easier, because though the political commentary was very partisan and harsh and so intense, I expected it. I knew it would be harsh, but it seemed that what I experienced running for office as a Republican and a Christian in Arkansas was worse. It was like a baseball game where the pitcher throws one at my head. I'm on the ground and I'm thinking, *Is that the best you got? That's your heat? Come on, prove to me you've got a better arm than that.*" Mike paused for a beat, in that humorous way that he has perfected, before adding, "Of course, I'd just think that to myself, I wouldn't say it, because he just might have proved it."

As we chuckled in response, Newt Gingrich seconded Mike's notion of not getting bent out of shape by the inevitable critiques. "Ignore external criticism unless it's making a difference or it rings true. Margaret Thatcher used to revel in the fact that she never read a newspaper or watched TV news because it would get her emotionally off balance. She also never read articles about herself, because she said she knew herself better than the people writing the articles did. Of course, she had staff who would read the newspapers, but you want a barrier between yourself and the emotional experience of worrying about criticism.

"So you try to be open to criticism internally, and to pay attention only to the external criticism that your people tell you is valid," was Newt's prescription. "You have to accept the fact that if you're going to be a defining leader, by definition the people you program against are going to be mad at you. It never used to worry me much that liberal Democrats went nuts, because they were right: we *were* taking power away from them, and with the help of the American people we *were* changing the Congress they thought they should run as a plantation."

"Pressure goes with the territory," admitted Tony Dungy. "When you accept a leadership position, you are going to accept everything that comes with it: the accolades, the fanfares, the thank-yous, the tough times, the extra work, the disappointment, the criticism. All of that comes with the job, and included with that is the pressure to make the right decision. That's probably the biggest pressure, when you are not sure what to do and you realize the decision you made is going to impact so many people in your organization.

"The outside pressure—what people think or what people say I should do—that has never bothered me. It's the pressure of whether I should do A or B when I'm not quite sure what is the best thing to do. I have to take all the information I have, gather input from all the people around me, and make a decision. For me, there comes a point where I just have to rely on praying about it and getting a feeling inside that this is the best thing to do. I have to say to the Lord, *I believe I'm making the right call.*"

The emphasis upon internal pressure was something that Laurie Beth Jones had experienced in leading and in consulting other leaders. "Pressure comes from conflicting desires, and if your only desire is to please God, then the pressure is not from the outside—it's really the internal pressure. *Am I going to do that? Stand here and do that? Or be pulled off?* I'm working with a client right now who is just an incredible human being, and in fact, I work with him because I want to hang around him to learn more. But he was just having a casual conversation the other day, and he said, 'I know where I'm going and I

Pressure goes with the territory.

know what my destiny is, and all this stuff about the economy and everything else can come and go. I know what I came here to do.' And there was such a peace about him, and you know, he's in the middle of a tumultuous industry, but there was a peace about him. I think the willingness to lose everything when you have nothing to lose—when you live in surrender, nothing is really yours unless it was given, not even your own life—makes it easier to take the pressure. People who are people-pleasers are never going to be satisfied. They are always going to be under pressure."

Michael Franzese cleared his throat in preparation for addressing the topic. "You know, Paul the apostle has had a very powerful impact on my life and particularly on my leadership. Paul said that if you're not criticized for your leadership skills and the things you say, then you're not an effective leader. People are always going to criticize decisions they don't like. You can't lead at the whim of the people; you have to lead people to do what's right, and part of leading well is to believe in what you're saying and then get even the doubters to go along, even if they're reluctant."

John Townsend tacked onto Michael's comment about the inevitability of being criticized if you're doing something significant. "Leadership, by definition, involves pressure. If there's no pressure, there's no need for a leader. So a leader who signs up for the job must normalize pressure and expect it rather than hoping it doesn't happen.

"The expectation helps, but you also need resourcing to handle the pressure. What that means is, first, you need to be grounded in very supportive relationships in your life so that when you fail or are misunderstood or there's a big mistake, you've got people who will cheer you up, encourage you, give you a dose of wisdom. You need people who will tell you, 'Attaboy, we are on your team no matter what,' so you can get back in the fray. You have to be connected with others.

"Secondly, you have to have experience. If a leader is thinking, *I want to take on a new position or get a promotion or take on a different industry,* he or she has to be able to handle the current pressures: strengthening decision-making muscles, dealing well with conflict, persevering, delaying gratification, continually heading for the goal, and so forth. To be able to handle your present circumstances increases your readiness to handle new things. In the future you are going to have an increase of pressure, so strengthen those muscles today."

Barry Black posited that in addition to normalizing pressure—expecting it, preparing for it, and having the resources in place to adequately handle it—there ought to be a spiritual side to how leaders respond to criticism and pressure.

"I think the way to deal with pressure is very simple: take the instructions of Scripture seriously and be a doer, not just a hearer, of those instructions. In Matthew 7:24-27, ending His Sermon on the Mount, Jesus talks about pressure. He talks about pressure on two homes—one built on a foundation of rock and the other on a foundation of sand. To me the moral of the story is not just to get the right foundation, but it is also to be aware that pressure will come to every life, regardless of what the foundation is like. But Jesus said, 'If you hear my sayings and do them, then your house will survive.' And there's another message from Him in John 16:33, which in the Greek actually uses the word *pressure*. The New King James Version says, 'In the world you will have tribulation; but be of good cheer, I have overcome the world.' The word that is translated 'tribulation' is *pressure* in the Greek, and 'be of good cheer' is actually *take courage*. So Jesus is saying, face your pressure with courage.

"If we're to be doers of the Word, then we should face pressure with courage. And Jesus ends by saying, 'Be of good cheer, I have overcome the world'—or, take courage, for I have overcome the world. Seeing things from an eternal perspective, I guess I would add that if Christ has overcome the world, then for a Christian leader that means eternity is my ultimate destiny. And if eternity is my ultimate destiny, suddenly the pressure of the times is not nearly as cataclysmic."

Those were certainly encouraging thoughts. They reminded me of my favorite verses in Ecclesiastes, where Solomon reminds us that most of what we experience and hope for in life is meaningless. What really matters is loving and obeying God. Or Jesus' words in Matthew 6, when He told His followers not to worry about tomorrow, because there are enough issues to deal with today. But my struggle in the face of crushing pressure was putting into practice the things that I knew intellectually and could recite at the drop of a hat. It was that traffic jam between my head and heart.

As I pondered those matters, it wasn't until Lou Taylor and Miles McPherson chimed in that I realized we had all embraced some assumptions in the course of our dialogue that may have been unwarranted. The pressure we feel might be of our own making and easily dismissed if we simply examine why we feel it. Lou was the first to articulate that viewpoint. "Sometimes pressure is brought on for unnecessary reasons, so I try to decide if this is something that I really need to be worried about. *Is this something that I should be anxious about? Is this something that needs to be done right now?* Just asking myself those questions helps me avoid getting to the point where pressure overtakes me and I fall apart."

She must have received a skeptical glance or two because she quickly added, "I mean, don't get me wrong. I have my days when I feel like Sybil chained to the piano, and I don't know what person will be walking in today. But for the most part, the result of asking those questions has been a greater sense of peace and even accomplishment. And having the right people in the position to do that helps."

Miles added his reflection on the matter. "I find that through pressure, God purifies my heart. How can a leader prepare for pressure? By handling pressure. By being in the fire. There is no other way."

There were murmurs of agreement with Miles's assessment of how to get ready for pressure. As the banter died down, Rich Stearns took the floor to suggest one of the opportunities that pressure and criticism provide to a leader. He spoke about turning an environment ripe for criticism and even hostility into an opportunity to move people beyond the immediate situation.

"I mentioned earlier that we had a salary freeze, and that was not a popular decision. In that case I didn't have time to consult everybody beforehand and get their buy-in. We had to do something urgently. But after the fact, we had an all-employee meeting where I tried to do a little vision casting. I asked them, 'Can you understand why I'm doing this? I'm not doing this for me. I'm not doing this to punish you. I'm doing this because our mission calls us to protect the most vulnerable. And I'm asking you to join me in this even though it hurts.'

"That was using the inspiration of our vision to get people on the same page. After that meeting I was told that a number of people went to HR and volunteered their salary increase for the whole year as a way to support the cause. I had said there was only going to be a three-month delay in salary increases, yet people voluntarily offered to give their salary increase for the whole year. Obviously some people embraced the mission, but that came out of turning what could have been a time for complaints into a time of reestablishing our commitment to the vision."

All of these stories and principles about criticism and pressure seemed to drive home the lesson that leading people is not a popularity contest. As one of our leaders had wisecracked, if you want friends, go to a sports club or church social; if you want to lead, then experiencing pressure and criticism—and reacting appropriately—are just part of the job. The inability to respond appropriately can undermine your opportunity and capacity to lead.

Leaders facilitate change, which generates resistance and criticism. Leaders set goals and must motivate and mobilize people to reach them, a process that creates pressure and pushback. Leaders must help people to know and do what's right, which stimulates controversy and disputes. Leadership is not for the faint of heart.

Our discussion reminded me that nothing worth creating comes without paying a price. For a leader, part of the price is enduring the emotional roller coaster of being on the receiving end of complaints and challenges, and the physical hardship of feeling the pressure to live up to expectations, even if it's only your own. You have to believe in the vision and in your ability to see it become a reality to turn your critics into fans and to relieve the pressure by performing up to standards.

CHAPTER 16

SKILLS AND DISCIPLINE

IT WAS HARD TO BELIEVE, but we were already near the end of the conference. Where had the time gone? I could have spent a few more days interacting with these great minds and hearts, drilling for more of the intellectual gold that seemed to gush out of these people as if they possessed a deep, unending supply of such wisdom.

With only the final session remaining, most of the experts who were not involved in the last session were packing up their notes and other belongings and heading to the bus that would take them back to the hotel, the airport, or wherever they were off to next. It was a sad parting. I sensed that some of them were reluctant to leave, as we'd had a good time learning from and getting to know each other. But everyone had other obligations to tend to, so we said our good-byes and refocused.

For me, the next task was leading the closing session on the big stage, a panel discussion involving seven of our guests. The topic that had been chosen for us had to do with the skills and disciplines a person needs to become a great leader. Normally nervous before I address any audience, I was not at all nervous this time; I simply had to facilitate the conversation among a cast of top-caliber leaders, not unlike what we had been doing in the greenroom over the past two days.

As the crowd returned to the auditorium from its final break, the team and I marched onstage and took our places under the blinding, hot lights that pretty much prevented us from being able to see the people to whom we'd be speaking. We sat behind a series of high-legged bar tables, facing the audience and trying to get comfortable on the stools that were arranged in a line behind the tables. We quickly tested the microphones and waited quietly for the stage manager to cue us. When he did, I welcomed people back for the final presentation and set up the discussion for everyone onstage and in the audience. We would focus on identifying and understanding the skills, competencies, and disciplines it takes for someone to maximize his or her leadership.

To no one in particular, I threw out the question "What skill is perhaps most necessary to be an effective leader?" I was shocked when an immediate response came back—in fact, the same response offered by six of the seven panelists!

"Listening" was the discipline they had identified. After the audience laughed at the single-mindedness of the group, I invited Ken Blanchard to kick off our consideration of the significance of listening.

"Tony Robbins gave me a great concept one time," he began, alluding to the bestselling self-help expert. "He said there are two kinds of listening. One is sorting by self and the other is sorting by others. People who are lousy listeners sort by self. If you say to them, 'It's a beautiful day,' they'll say, 'Yeah, but you should have seen the weather in Michigan where I was yesterday.' They take the conversation away from you. They sort by self.

"People who sort by others," he continued, "keep the ball in the other person's court. If you say to them, 'Isn't it a beautiful day?' people who sort by others would respond, 'What does a beautiful day do for you?' If you reply, 'Well, it just gives me energy,' then they'd ask, 'What happens when you get that kind of energy?'

"I think that kind of listening can be taught, but the person's first got to be humble enough to listen and hear that he or she has a problem and to really want to change. I've worked with top managers, and a lot of people don't think you should set goals related to behavior. I disagree. If the feedback on a guy is that he's a lousy listener, then we ought to identify that as a behavioral goal he's going to have. The first group that he needs to talk to about this is his management team. He could approach the team and say, 'Look, I've gotten feedback from you and others that I'm a lousy listener. What I want is to put structure in here when we're having meetings so that I can't make any comment about anything anybody says until I tell the last speaker what they said and they agree that's what they said.' It's just an old Carl Rogers trick to teach people to keep quiet.

"Paul Meyers once had a financial officer who was just terrific financially, but she was a real pain on new ideas. She would throw a wet blanket on everything. Paul really liked what she could do financially, but he called her in and said, 'You're one of the best I've ever had financially, but your capacity to put a wet blanket on new ideas is career damaging. From now on, if you're in a meeting with me or any of our team and a new idea comes up, you can't say anything negative. I'm putting you in charge of "green light thinking." You have to tell us all the reasons we *should* do that.' After a while she lost her habit of putting things down. The whole thing about listening is to listen with the attitude that you could have your mind changed."

Ken paused to glance around the auditorium to gauge people's connection with his story, but the stage lights pretty much blinded us, so he continued. "Another important thing is knowing the difference between listening and deciding. One of the reasons a lot of people don't listen is that when you give them feedback, they start thinking about all the problems of implementing what you just said and then they tell you why it's going to be hard to do that, rather than just asking for more information about how it could work so that later on they can decide whether they want to do something with the idea.

"One of my favorite stories about listening," Ken revealed, "is when I was in a mall a few years ago. I was walking behind a woman and her son, who must have been ten or eleven years old. They passed by a sporting goods store that had a beautiful red bicycle in the window. The kid stopped dead in his tracks and said to his mother, 'Boy, would I like a bicycle like that.' She went absolutely berserk. She started to scream and yell, 'I can't believe you. I just got you a new bike for Christmas, and here it's March and you already want another one. Well I'm not gonna get you one.' I thought she was going to level this kid.

"I wish somebody had taught her the difference between listening and deciding, because if she had listened, she would have said, 'Honey, what do you like about that bike?' Maybe he would have said, 'Well, look at those streamers coming out of the handlebars there.' Well, that's a pretty cheap birthday present, you know? 'What else do you like about it?' 'Well, I have a really narrow seat, and I'd kind of like that big seat.' Well, that's interesting. And if you listen to the kid, then you could even ask later on, 'Honey, why do you think I can't get you a whole new bike?' That kid's not stupid. He'll say, 'Mom, I just got one for Christmas.' So I tell you, listening is probably one of the most important skills and one we could all use. I love the whole concept of leading with your ears. I heard that phrase recently; it has a nice ring to it."

Through the blaze of lights, I thought I saw a bunch of parents slump in their chairs while Ken told that story, but it seemed that the audience was picking up on Ken's message. The positive reaction encouraged our other leader blessed with homespun wisdom and humor to give his views about the importance of listening.

"Well, first of all, I never learned anything—and I'm an old man—by talking," began Lou Holtz. "The only times I've ever learned anything were by listening or reading. Now, with your staff, you have to realize there's a time to listen and there's a time not to listen. I've been on the football field, and we have a minimum amount of time in the game, so I'm not interested in listening to a player tell me something. I'm interested in getting him to play. Now, if you come into my office, I'll sit and listen to anything you want to say. But there's a time for you to talk and a time for you to listen and there's a time for you to execute.

"It's the same thing in a staff meeting. When we were in a staff meeting and I would bring something up, I would listen to every coach in that room. I'd go around the room, and everybody had an opportunity to voice his opinion. I wouldn't say a lot; I'd just make notes to myself. When they were done I would say, 'This is what we're going to do and here's why,' and I would explain my decisions after having heard their ideas. And I would not feel that if we had rejected someone's idea once before, we had to accept it the next time. We were all there for one purpose, and that was to win. Our focus was to win games and to graduate students. If you're running a business, all you're trying to do is satisfy the needs of the customer and the needs of the stockholders, period. Everything else is irrelevant. You don't worry about egos, you don't worry about feelings; your purpose is to satisfy your goals.

"So I would listen to people, but when I made a decision, we weren't going to rehash it. Hey, you've had your say. I understand what you're saying. I understand why you believe what you do. But I'm making the decision. I've listened to everybody. Here is the decision, here's where we're going, here's why we're going there, and we aren't going to discuss this anymore. And when we walk out of this room, everybody is 100 percent completely sold on the fact that this is the proper thing to do. Loyalty is an absolute necessity. And loyalty is not just saying yes: it's voicing your opinion vehemently and strongly on things you believe in that meeting but accepting the final decision as your own. When we walk out of that meeting, we are one voice and one accord."

My interpretation of his words was that listening to everyone's thoughts and picking those that advance your vision doesn't mean that leading people becomes a democracy. Sometimes I have been frustrated that people in leadership roles have felt compelled to concede to the popular view. I appreciated Coach's warning that it's reasonable to hear everyone out, but that the role of the leader is to make the final call. Lou's words opened the door for Rich Stearns's thoughts on the matter. He resonated with Coach's note that giving people an opportunity to voice their views and influence the final outcome is a valuable practice.

"It's important for a leader to listen to multiple points of view," he stated. "Be willing to listen—and don't just pretend you're listening, but actually listen to what people think and gather information from different points of view. Inherent in that is making your people feel safe, letting them see that it's okay to disagree and to speak up. It's critical to build a culture of truth-telling and speaking the truth to power and speaking the truth in love.

"Years ago I was between jobs; I was unemployed, and I was working with an outplacement counselor. He said something to me I've never forgotten, which I think applies to both leaders and followers. He said, 'Try this with your attitude. If your phone rings, or if someone walks into your office with a question, make your first answer, "How can I help you?" If you have the attitude that you're there to help others succeed and to help others solve their problems, you're going to be a great leader and you're going to be a great follower.' When people come to you with an issue, if you ask, 'How can I help you? How can I help make this better? How can I add value? What can I do to make your job easier and give you a higher chance of success?' you will be showing a great attitude, whether you're a follower or a leader."

The role of the leader is to make the final call.

That approach impressed Laurie Beth Jones, who asserted that a leader's attitude and objective when listening makes a big difference in the value of doing so.

"So many leaders get up there and they think that it's sheer wind power that is going to persuade people. But it's really by listening deeply that you begin to understand what the value set is and what the needs of the people around you are, and then you are able to persuade them to move in a new direction.

"Perhaps the most important quality that a leader can possess is appreciative inquiry and listening without a preconceived agenda. Imagine how the world could change if people began by listening and understanding what the other person wants before they run them over with a bulldozer. If you listen, it not only prevents them from getting run over by the bulldozer, but it also encourages them to actually get on the bulldozer and get twelve of their friends to help out. It's a lost art. To get there, the first thing is to recognize the beauty of each person's personality type and address the recognition that comes with that. If you don't incorporate other people's values, then you are not going to have anything that is sustained over a long period of time."

Our leaders had alluded to how and why listening was a necessity, but I wondered exactly how one does that. After all, my research found that most leaders think they are good enough at listening. What does successful listening look like? What does it take? Barry Black offered one approach.

"I think that the way you listen to people is through the intending process, as the counselors would say. There's an acrostic that is sometimes used called SOLER. Are you familiar with that?" Barry asked. I admitted that I had never been exposed to that system and asked what it was about.

"*S* stands for 'sit squarely'; *O* means you should have an 'open posture'— no crossed legs or crossed hands." I tried to unobtrusively uncross my legs while looking him squarely in the eye, hoping he wouldn't notice my attempt to recover. "*L* is for 'leaning forward.' *E* is about making 'eye contact.' *R* is for 'rephrasing' what people have said, paraphrasing back to them what you think you heard, just for clarification. If you use those attending tactics in listening aggressively to people, or active listening, as it is sometimes called, you will be able to intuit things, and that's the hearing of what is not being said. And then, in your paraphrasing back to them, many times you can validate whether or not you're hearing what has not been said correctly by including that in your paraphrase, and they will respond to and build on that."

That was one of the most succinct lessons I'd had in a complex art. Barry gave a further bit of advice on the art of listening.

"You know, when you listen, you must not only hear what people are saying, but you must also learn to hear what they aren't saying. Many times that message is more germane than what they're actually saying."

I turned to John Townsend, who wasn't saying much of anything yet. I hoped there was no hidden message in that! I asked him for his thoughts on helping leaders become better listeners. After affirming Barry's ideas, John added more grist for the mill.

"Let me add two factors," he started, putting me at ease. "One is that the leader must be able to measure value added by listening. A lot of leaders think they're too busy to be bothered—they've got a business to run. But if you look at the research that has been done, you find you will meet more goals and quotas if you listen well, and you will miss more opportunities and overlook problems you need to deal with if you don't listen well. So leaders need to see there is value in listening, because it adds to their expected outcome and goals.

"Number two, I really believe in role-playing. I believe that, since leaders often don't come by that skill naturally, they need to see it. What they see and experience is what they remember. Often, if they can be with someone— a coach, a consultant, or someone who is good with these matters—and they role-play a situation, then the lights come on. If I do this, I might give the person eye contact and ask, 'How was that for you? How did that feel?' After the person responds I might say, 'Tell me more about that,' or 'That must have been difficult for you.' This is how some people open up, and I find out what is really going on with them. Simple role-playing can be really powerful for a leader."

I asked what other skills and disciplines leaders need to reach their potential. Rich Stearns saw a relationship between the conversation on listening and the need for leaders to understand more about themselves and the effect of their position.

"A leader needs self-awareness, being acutely aware of how others perceive him or her. I tend to use humor a lot to make people feel comfortable or at ease around me. I've learned that when you're the CEO, people are often terrified in your presence. It doesn't matter what your personality is; when people walk into a meeting with the CEO, they're on their guard, they're nervous, they're worried about their performance. If you can put them at ease by showing that you're just a regular person, that you know how to laugh at yourself and create a comfortable environment, then people are much more emboldened to candidly share their views and their beliefs.

"Leaders have to be very aware of the power they wield. When you're at the bottom of the hierarchical ladder, sometimes you have to shout to be heard, because you don't have any title or you don't have authority. But when you are the CEO or a top leader, you can speak softly and it sounds like a shout to someone. So when you criticize someone, you have to be very careful about being too blunt or cutting, because whatever you say will be amplified ten times just because you're the president. You have to adapt your style to realize that it's not just you, the person, speaking; it's the position that you hold that's speaking."

Someone pointed out that sometimes leaders feel so comfortable in their roles that they lose sight of how others feel in their presence. That brought Rich to a related point.

"Another element of self-awareness is understanding how you're seen by others in the organization. How are you perceived by your peers? Are you perceived as a collaborator, as a team player, or are you perceived as partisan and divisive? Are you perceived as helpful and constructive or as resistant and putting up barriers? And how are you perceived by your subordinates? How are your words received by your subordinates?"

After a couple of side comments were made about sensitivity to image and position, John interjected some insights on another aspect of self-awareness.

"Leaders have to have a certain amount of self-control. In fact, if you look in the Bible, self-control is listed as one of the fruits of the Spirit; it's in there and important enough to say that it matters. Every leader must develop discipline and structure and a sense of focus, and be able to say no to things that aren't what he or she should focus on. Along with that, a leader needs to have some kind of an ongoing analysis of his or her values. We always need to be coming back to our anchors. It's so easy to lose touch with those things. In fact, if you look at research among visionary leaders, they are the ones who always, no matter what the conversation is about, bring us back to the core values. They help us to refocus, to kind of reset. The discipline of coming back to the essential values is key.

"And another one that is huge, and it's probably not done as much in leadership as it should be, is focusing on personal growth. This is the discipline of submitting yourself to a process where you're looking at your life, your values, your spirituality, your relationships, and you're submitting to other people and letting them scrutinize these on a regular basis, not just giving them a one-time look. Ideally, somebody's always giving you feedback about life and you're submitting yourself to that process, whether you receive positive or negative feedback."

Barry built onto John's thoughts. "Absolutely. Leaders need to pursue the discipline of maintaining fitness in the physical, intellectual, and spiritual areas. Many times we might be good at one but poor at another. I remember seeing a photograph of a great religious leader in the newspaper, and he obviously had a powerful devotional life, but he had triple chins. So this ability to maintain whole fitness, it's not just in the spiritual area, but also in the intellectual and the physical areas."

"That's what I'd refer to as integration," replied John, "meaning I believe God designed us to have different parts or aspects that should be working together smoothly. An integrated leader has the abilities we talked about earlier: the ability to lead and relate to people on a deeper level and understand them, the ability to be clear and defined, the ability to fail well. If all of those abilities are working well together, they are integrated."

Laurie Beth connected the past few statements to one of the disciplines she strives to develop in the leaders she coaches.

"Leaders are naturally really good at exciting people and releasing resources to do things. But one of their common weaknesses is getting grounded in data and research, really knowing the facts before they launch out on a campaign. Jesus said you shouldn't start something without counting the costs, but we see that all the time in leadership."

John noted that her concept of making sure the leader is grounded in reality is connected to his desire that leaders be able to welcome challenging information.

"Lots of leaders don't want to hear bad news," John confirmed, "so they surround themselves with people who will give them good news, even when it's not true news. I was talking to an executive earlier this week about consulting with his organization, and he said one thing I can help him with is that he requires his team to write reports, and they are terrified because they don't want to disappoint and upset him. They are afraid that if they write the truth they will let him down, so all they tell him is how great things are at the same time that they tell each other how bad things are. He wants to break that cycle. He's a good person and he sees the problem, but that's an important discipline that leaders don't naturally possess."

I pointed out that if one of the primary functions of leaders is to understand reality so they can change it for the better, that kind of truth-telling is crucial to success. One of the avenues to doing so, according to Barry, was being self-controlled enough to give God His rightful place in the process and wait for Him to provide the guidance that the leader needs to carry out the vision.

"Waiting on God is one discipline that many leaders have difficulty mastering," Barry explained. "It's the Abraham and Hagar situation: God is not moving fast enough." That was one of the things I'd come to appreciate about the chaplain; he said a lot of the things we are sometimes afraid to admit to ourselves. What leader who follows Christ hasn't been frustrated at times because it seemed as if God was behind the pace—our pace?

But to Rich, the challenge of slowing down and taking our cues from God raised the issue of priorities.

"The most effective leaders," Rich observed, "are good at constantly pushing away the things that consume them but that are not adding value at the end of the day, and they try to spend more and more time on those things that do add value.

"I'll give you an example from my time at Lenox. I recognized that the success of Lenox depended very heavily on having new products that became hits. If you are a recording artist, success is having a top-ten hit on the charts, a hit album. If you're an author, having a *New York Times* bestselling book is what you want. Lenox, in a sense, is like many other businesses in that if you have products that capture the public's support and a lot of people want to buy them, you can do a lot of other things wrong in your business and still succeed because you've got the updraft of a line of successful products being introduced in the market. Tableware is essentially a fashion business where you introduce new products and new fashions for the new season. You try to capture the imagination of brides and women who buy these things.

"So recognizing that, I asked myself, *How should I spend my time? How much time should I spend in meetings about information technology? How much time should I spend in meetings about legal issues and financial issues? How much time should I spend in meetings that are about product development, marketing strategy, and new product designs?* I intentionally tried to spend more and more of my time in meetings that were related to product development design, marketing research, and those kinds of things, because I really believed that they would pay dividends at the end of the day. When I would look back at the end of the year and assess what made the year successful or unsuccessful, it was almost always whether our product lines were strong or weak.

"It was a little bit unusual for a CEO serving in that context, but I would sit through two-day- or three-day-long product development meetings, looking at every new design, every new concept, working through the issues of manufacturing and marketing. Those are matters that most CEOs would just delegate to the specialists. But by being at those meetings, I lifted up the importance of the process to everybody else in the organization. The message was, 'This is the most important thing we do. This is the lifeblood of our business.' And then I tried to remove from my plate the things that drained my energy and didn't really change the bottom line much."

That reminded me of something that Bob Dees had said in the greenroom, when he was telling stories about what it was like being a leader in combat. I asked Bob to share some of his ideas about the significance of a leader's presence in the midst of important moments.

"Often, especially when it's early in a leadership tenure, people question whether the leader cares or is competent. Those questions linger until the leader makes his or her first major decision or everyone encounters their first crisis together. That's when the character of the leader is defined, either for better or worse. Either the people are with the leader or not, and he or she can either lead them to the gates of hell or not, depending on how he or she responds.

"On October 31, 1998, I was new in command," Bob recalled, his eyes intense with the memory. "I was out hitting golf balls during my downtime when a call came in. They said an armored personnel carrier, returning from guard duty in the demilitarized zone right on the edge of North Korea, had driven off a bridge into the river, and it plunged ninety feet down. Divers were there trying to get to them but a long time had already elapsed. So I immediately got in a helicopter and went there, but by then it was already pitch black.

"The colonel in charge was a wonderful gentleman, a real student of soldiers and leadership. He is one of those leaders who doesn't appear to be a natural leader at first glance. I got there and talked with him and some of his other leaders. One of them was one of his battalion leaders, a man who now heads the leadership department at West Point. I assessed the situation and simply told them, 'We're going to make it; it's going to be okay.' These frantic leaders were feeling burdened by a lot of things—what to think and say; what this situation would mean for their careers, which they saw flashing in front of their eyes; what it meant for the men they were leading. You can imagine the inner turmoil. With a few simple words, we were able to take it all off the table. I said, 'Now let's get to work and figure this out, and work the options.' I've had it played back to me by them a number of times, and they told me that it was not what I said, but what I didn't say that impacted them."

And, I pointed out, it was also huge that Bob chose to be present with his men at the time of crisis. He cared enough to jump into the midst of their angst and need, and provided the steadying hand that they required at that moment. With characteristic humility, Bob responded to that comment.

"You need to be able to lead with calmness and clarity in a crisis, but powerful leaders also capture the emotion of the moment as well. Leaders should not manipulate people's emotions, but they should be sufficiently transparent to show empathy, compassion, righteous anger, and passion for the common cause to tap into the human emotions experienced by the team they lead.

"As a young lieutenant, every once in a while I found myself tearing up in front of the troops when we accomplished something great or when we'd had a great loss. And I was always embarrassed about that. One day one of my junior officers came in and said, 'Sir, it's okay to cry.' People engaged in the art of leadership have got to put their hearts as well as their heads into the process. Yes, there has to be a balance, but many senior leaders err based on the false impression that showing emotion is showing weakness and a leader should never do that. But a slight touch of vulnerability is very positive in leading people."

As our time drew to a close, Coach Holtz offered a parting thought for the audience, playing off the authenticity of General Dees.

"You see, this goes back to what our core values are. You have to care about people. Regardless of how talented someone may be, if you can't trust him, if he isn't going to do the right thing, if he isn't committed to excellence, if he doesn't care—you've got a problem. You have got to care about your family and about your people.

"I was coaching and we were getting ready to play Michigan, and we had a boy who went into a coma. At that point the Michigan game meant absolutely nothing to me."

I stopped Coach for a moment, interrupting him to inform the football illiterates among us that a Notre Dame–Michigan game in the 1990s was the pinnacle of college football significance. Hearing the coach of the country's top team at the time describe such a game as meaning "absolutely nothing" was virtually, well, blasphemous! But, of course, Coach was making a very significant point about maintaining perspective and loving the people you lead.

Unfazed by the interruption—or perhaps just incapable of believing that any responsible American would be unaware of the magnitude of a Notre Dame–Michigan game—Coach continued. "What was important was my family needed me. I try to make sure people honor my core values. It's not complicated. I'm not the brightest bulb on the Christmas tree, but I try to keep life simple so not only do I understand, but the people I'm dealing with understand as well. Leaders sometimes forget the importance of fundamentals. Nobody likes to play "Chopsticks." Everybody wants to play Chopin. But it's the fundamentals that allow you to reach your goals. It's the fundamentals that enable you to build an organization. And there are fundamentals involved in having relationships with people. One of those is caring for your people."

Looking at the seven people seated on the stools to my right, I beamed at them in admiration. This Mount Rushmore of leadership could have taken any hill, any battle thrown at them. What an honor to be able to capture their wisdom and absorb their passion for leading. All of the leaders who had participated in the conference fit that bill. Theirs was a level of leadership that I hoped to move closer to as time went on and more experiences afforded me the chance to apply the insights they had imparted.

After thanking them for their contributions and then making some wrap-up comments for the benefit of the crowd, I dismissed them, and our team hoofed it back to the greenroom. Once there, we exchanged handshakes and hugs, traded e-mail addresses and phone numbers, and promised to stay in touch.

But with a disappointment borne in reality, I knew that, for the most part, that was not likely to happen. These were great leaders in high demand. They had battles to fight and victories to win, people to nurture and organizations to grow. As Rich had said during our panel discussion, they were focused on their priorities.

These were people, like all great leaders, busy creating the future.

NEXT STEPS

SOMETIMES AFTER SPEAKING at a conference, I find that the adrenaline rush subsides and I feel wiped out. That was how I was feeling on the way to the airport to fly home after the Master Leader Conference. After months of preparation and two days of unique and exhilarating experiences, there was plenty to reflect on now that the adventure was but a footnote in history.

Peering absentmindedly out the backseat window of the taxi, I wondered what the thousands who had attended the event went home with. What ideas had met them at their points of need? Which ideas had challenged them to rise to new heights? Who had said something that left an indelible impression on their minds and hearts? How would those who attended the conference change—become better leaders, better followers, better people?

Actually, those were the questions I needed to ask myself. More than anybody else in that cavernous building, I had reason to feel stretched and challenged. And after gathering all the information that was laid at my feet by the best in the business, it was now my responsibility to do something with that priceless resource. To do anything less would have been bad stewardship of the experience and a slap in the face to the mentors who had good-naturedly answered all my questions and provided whatever wisdom was theirs to impart.

As we sat in traffic, I pulled a notepad out of my travel bag and began to outline the major topics we had touched on in the greenroom and on the main stage. Then I grouped them together and came up with what I felt were the sixteen most significant dimensions the conference had addressed. Here is what was on my list.

1. Defining leadership and what makes somebody a leader
2. Defining leadership success
3. Knowing how to identify, communicate, and get commitment to vision as well as determining core values
4. Using core values to establish a viable organizational culture
5. Identifying people who are leaders and implementing practices that nurture their development
6. Figuring out whom to hire, how to set them up for success and protect myself from harm, and when and how to part ways with them
7. Finding touchstones for leading effectively: knowing what to look for and how to measure performance
8. Earning and maintaining people's trust
9. Engaging in positive confrontation, resolving conflict, and negotiating appropriately
10. Developing character traits that honor God, serve people, and empower self
11. Building up followers so they can be effective in collaborating with other leaders and with other followers
12. Creating teams of leaders whose gifts and abilities complement those of the other team members

13. Establishing and retaining the moral authority to lead, as well as integrating one's faith and faith-based principles into leadership decisions and practices

14. Knowing how power is derived and how to use it appropriately

15. Expecting, adapting to, and making the most of criticism and pressure

16. Identifying and honing the skills and disciplines required to perform at a high level of leadership

While the experience was still fresh in my mind, I planned to use the plane ride home to jot down the key insights and challenges garnered at the event. I would then convert those revelations into a personal action plan that would guide me toward becoming a better leader. In the past, this exercise had helped transform interesting conference experiences into life-changing events. And if there was ever a life-changing event for me, it had to be the Master Leader Conference. I owed it to God, to myself, to the people I lead, and to the coaches who gave me their best insights to apply the experience in that way.

Let me suggest that even though you experienced the Master Leader Conference through my filter, it might be beneficial for you to do the same thing. If you'd like to, feel free to use the sixteen topical dimensions I listed above to help you organize the insights that you drew from the experience, vicarious as it was for you. If you have the privilege and responsibility of leading others, use the information you gleaned as a means of taking your leadership abilities and commitments to the next level. After all, biologists have learned that every living organism is in one of two states: growth or decay. There is no such thing as maintenance; standing still is equivalent to decay. Given what was provided by the master leaders, neither you nor I have any excuse for decaying.

Be determined to grow every day in your leadership capacities. I'm sure the guidance provided by the master leaders can boost your capacity.

ABOUT THE MASTER LEADERS

John Ashcroft served as United States attorney general during the first term of President George W. Bush, from 2001 until 2005. John was previously the governor of Missouri (1985–1993), a U.S. senator from Missouri (1995–2001), and as both the attorney general of Missouri (1976–1985) and the state auditor (1973–1975). He graduated from Yale University, then received a JD degree from the University of Chicago in 1967. After law school, he briefly taught business law and worked as an administrator at Southwest Missouri State University. He currently leads a strategic consulting firm, the Ashcroft Group, LLC, located in Washington DC. He also serves as Distinguished Professor of Law and Government at Regent University School of Law.

Colleen Barrett is the former president and corporate secretary of Southwest Airlines. She has been with the company since its inception in 1971. She has been associated with Southwest's founder, Herb Kelleher, since 1967 when she went to work as his legal secretary. Since March of 1978 she has served as secretary of Southwest, as vice president of administration from 1986 through 1990, and executive vice president from 1990 through 2001. Colleen has been consistently listed among the most powerful business-women in the United States. She stepped down as president and corporate secretary of Southwest in July 2008 but will remain an employee of the corporation through July 2013.

Warren Bennis is widely regarded as a pioneer of the contemporary field of leadership studies. He is currently University Professor, Distinguished Professor of Business Administration, and founding chairman of the Leadership Institute at the University of Southern California. His articles and books have defined the field and helped to change leadership practice into a less hierarchical, more democratic and adaptive art. In addition to teaching at USC, Harvard University, and Boston University, Warren has been an adviser to four United States presidents and other public figures, has consulted for numerous *Fortune* 500 companies, and served as the president of the University of Cincinnati. His book *An Invented Life* was nominated for a Pulitzer Prize. Among the best known of his twenty-nine books are the bestselling *Leaders* and *On Becoming a Leader*, both of which have been translated into twenty-one languages.

Barry Black is the chaplain of the United States Senate, elected to that position in 2003. He became the first African American, the first Seventh-day Adventist, and the first military chaplain to hold the office of chaplain to the United States Senate. He previously served for over twenty-seven years as a chaplain in the United States Navy, rising to the rank of rear admiral (UH) and ending his career as the chief of navy chaplains. He officially retired from the navy on August 15, 2003. In addition to earning master's degrees in divinity, counseling, and management, he has received a doctorate in ministry and a doctor of philosophy degree in psychology. Among

Chaplain Black's awards are the NAACP Renowned Service Award for his contribution to equal opportunity and civil rights, and the Benjamin Elijah Mays Distinguished Leadership Award from the Morehouse School of Religion.

Jimmy Blanchard served as CEO of Synovus from 1971 until being named chairman of the board in July 2005. His tenure spanned the periods of greatest growth in the firm's history as it blossomed into a $33 billion financial services company providing a diverse set of products and services. Synovus topped *Fortune* magazine's list of the 100 best companies to work for and has been recognized in its Hall of Fame for consecutive appearances on the list since its inception in 1998. Synovus was also named as one of America's most admired companies. Jimmy placed tremendous emphasis on leadership education at Synovus, focusing on servant leadership principles. He retired as chairman of Synovus in 2006. He earned a bachelor's degree in business administration and a law degree from the University of Georgia.

Ken Blanchard sparked a management revolution with his book *The One Minute Manager* (coauthored with Spencer Johnson), which has sold over 13 million copies and has been translated into thirty-seven languages. Blanchard is the "chief spiritual officer" of the Ken Blanchard Companies, an international management training and consulting firm that he and his wife, Marjorie Blanchard, cofounded in 1979. Ken cofounded, with Phil Hodges, Lead Like Jesus, a ministry committed to glorifying God by inspiring and equipping people to lead like Jesus. He has coauthored over thirty other bestselling books. Among many accolades, Blanchard has been honored as one of the world's top ten leadership professionals. Ken completed a BS degree in government and philosophy at Cornell University, an MA in sociology and counseling at Colgate University, and a PhD in education administration and leadership at Cornell University. He serves as a Cornell

University trustee emeritus and visiting professor at the Cornell University School of Hotel Administration.

Kirbyjon Caldwell is the pastor of the Windsor Village United Methodist Church, a 14,000-member megachurch in Houston, Texas. After college, Kirbyjon worked as an investment banker on Wall Street and in Houston before sensing a call to full-time ministry. After completing a seminary degree, he was appointed the senior pastor of the Windsor Village United Methodist Church in 1982 when the church had only twenty-five members. While leading Windsor Village, he transformed the church into an all-purpose community help center. To accommodate the size of the congregation, the church purchased a former Kmart in one of the most blighted parts of Houston and renovated it into the Power Center, which includes worship space, a school, a medical clinic, satellite classrooms for a local community college, low-cost office space, a bank, and various charities. The mission of the Power Center is to create jobs in the low-income neighborhood and to teach members of the neighborhood how to create wealth. Kirbyjon has been a director on the Continental Airlines board of directors since 1999 and was one of President George W. Bush's most influential spiritual advisers. Kirbyjon received his BS in economics from Carleton College, his MBA from the Wharton School of Business at the University of Pennsylvania, and his MDiv from the Perkins School of Theology at Southern Methodist University.

Ben Carson is the director of pediatric neurosurgery at Johns Hopkins Hospital, a position he has held since he was thirty-three years old. In 1987, Ben and a team of more than seventy physicians, surgeons, and nurses made medical history with a twenty-two-hour operation at Johns Hopkins to successfully separate a pair of conjoined twins. In 1997, Ben went to South Africa where he worked with a fifty-member team in the successful, twenty-eight-hour operation to separate eleven-month-old Zambian twin boys who were joined at the head. He sits on many boards, including those of Kellogg, Costco, and Yale University. He was also the president and cofounder of the Carson Scholars Fund, which recognizes young people of all backgrounds for exceptional academic and humanitarian accomplishments. A television movie about his life, *Gifted Hands: The Ben Carson Story*, premiered on TNT in 2009, with Academy Award winner Cuba Gooding Jr. in the lead role. Ben was awarded the Presidential Medal of Freedom in 2008.

Sam Chand is a former pastor, college president, and chancellor, and now serves as president emeritus of Beulah Heights University. Raised in a pastor's home in India, he later attended Beulah Heights University while working there as a janitor, cook, and dishwasher. After graduating, he worked in various positions before returning to the school to become its president. Under his leadership Beulah Heights University became the country's largest predominantly African American Bible college. Sam has authored eight books and consults with many leaders and organizations around the world. He has an honorary doctor of divinity from Heritage Bible College, a master of arts in biblical counseling from Grace Theological Seminary, and a bachelor of arts in biblical education from Beulah Heights University.

Henry Cloud is a clinical psychologist with broad experience in private practice, leadership consulting, and media. He is well known for his two-million-selling book, *Boundaries*, cowritten with John Townsend, and has written over twenty other books with a total of four million copies in print. Henry cofounded Minirth-Meier ClinicWest and served as its clinical codirector for ten years, operating treatment centers in thirty-five cities in the western United States. He is president of Cloud-Townsend Resources and runs a private practice with John Townsend in Newport Beach, California. He has philanthropic interests in the area of homelessness, the inner city, and Third World missions and development. Henry has a bachelor of science degree in psychology from Southern Methodist University and a PhD in clinical psychology from Biola University.

Bob Dees is a retired major general of the U.S. Army. After leaving the army, he was executive director of defense strategies at Microsoft before becoming executive director of the military ministry division of Campus Crusade for Christ International, which he currently leads. His latest initiative with Military Ministry centers around preventing and healing the hidden wounds of war in our nation's warriors and their families. General Dees served in a wide variety of command and staff positions in the military. He has commanded airborne, air assault, and mechanized infantry forces from the platoon through division levels. Bob has received numerous awards and decorations for his meritorious service. He earned his bachelor of science from the U.S. Military Academy (West Point) and holds a master of science degree in operations research and systems analysis from the Naval Postgraduate School. His also received substantial military education and was a research fellow at the Royal College of Defence Studies in London.

Tony Dungy is a former professional football player and coach in the NFL. After working as an assistant coach, he became head coach of the Tampa Bay Buccaneers and then the Indianapolis Colts. In 2007 he became the first African American head coach to win the Super Bowl. A year later he set a new NFL record for consecutive play-off appearances by a head coach and announced his retirement as coach of the Colts at the conclusion of the season. Tony has earned widespread respect both on and off the field for his strong commitment to ethical standards and behavior. He has been active in many community service organizations in the cities in which he has coached, initiated a mentoring program for young people called Mentors for Life, and continues to assist many other charitable programs. He is the author of three books that have been on the *New York Times* bestsellers list, including two that reached number one. As an undergraduate he attended the University of Minnesota, and he has an honorary doctorate from Indiana Wesleyan University.

Michael Franzese, from Brooklyn, New York, is the son of reputed Colombo underboss John "Sonny" Franzese, and joined the Colombo crime family as a young adult. He rose to become a caporegime, or captain, in the family and masterminded lucrative gasoline bootlegging rackets. *Fortune* magazine listed Michael as number eighteen on its list of the fifty most wealthy and powerful mafia bosses. According to a federal report, Franzese made more money for a crime family than anyone since legendary mobster Al Capone. Michael was involved in many business ventures, from operating automobile dealerships to producing movies. After becoming a Christian, he left the Colombo family and organized crime and was sent to prison for his role in the gasoline rackets. After completing his sentence, he created a foundation for helping youth and became a motivational speaker, frequently speaking to church groups, as well as to professional and student athletes about the dangers of gambling. His autobiography, *Blood Covenant*, has been a bestseller. In Martin Scorsese's heralded film *Goodfellas*, Michael is portrayed as the character Mickey Franzese.

Newt Gingrich served as the Speaker of the United States House of Representatives from 1995 to 1999. He was the *Time* magazine Person of the Year in 1995 for his role in leading the Republican revolution in the House. A college history professor, political leader, and author, Gingrich was elected to eleven terms in the House before he resigned both his House seat and role as Speaker. Newt has remained active in public policy matters as a senior fellow at the conservative think tank American Enterprise Institute; by founding the Center for Health Transformation; as a distinguished visiting fellow at the conservative think tank the Hoover Institute; as a commentator on television news shows; and as a founder of American Solutions for Winning the Future and the think tank American Solutions. He received a BA from Emory University, and an MA and a PhD from Tulane University. He has written several books about politics and cultural issues, in addition to several volumes of historical fiction.

Seth Godin is an author of business books and a popular speaker. He popularized the topic of permission marketing. A serial entrepreneur, he started his first business at age fourteen. After college, he worked in the software, publishing, and online marketing industries. He served as the first vice president of direct marketing at Yahoo! before launching out on his own again. He developed ChangeThis, a Web site aimed at spreading ideas through PDF files; and Squidoo, a community Web site allowing users to create pages for subjects of interest, which has become one of the most visited sites in the world. Seth is the author of a dozen books, including bestsellers such as *Purple Cow, The Dip, Tribes,* and *Permission Marketing.* His free e-book, *Unleashing the Ideavirus,* has been described as "the most popular e-book ever written." He consults with many leaders and businesses around the world. Seth graduated from Tufts University with a bachelor's degree in computer science and philosophy and earned his MBA in marketing from Stanford Business School.

Wilson Goode was the first African American mayor of Philadelphia, serving from 1984 to 1992. Prior to that he had served as the first black commissioner for the state's Public Utility Commission, and managing director for the city of Philadelphia. Since his time as mayor, Wilson has held midlevel positions in the U.S. Department of Education, become a minister, and taught at Eastern University. He currently serves as a senior adviser to Public/Private Ventures where he oversees Amachi, a mentoring program for children of incarcerated parents. He earned his undergraduate degree from Morgan State University; a master's degree in government administration from the University of Pennsylvania; and a doctor of ministry at Palmer Theological Seminary.

Jon Gordon is one of the emerging voices in the leadership field. He is a speaker and consultant, and is the author of the international bestseller *The Energy Bus.* He works with many sports organizations (e.g., NFL, PGA), government agencies (e.g., FBI), businesses (e.g., Campbell Soup,

Northwestern Mutual, Publix Super Markets, and JP Morgan Chase), and leaders in education (e.g., The Principal's Partnership and National Association of School Principals). Jon is a graduate of Cornell University and holds a master's degree from Emory University.

Lou Holtz has been an NCAA football and NFL head coach, television commentator (CBS Sports and ESPN), and motivational speaker. Known for his quick wit and ability to inspire players, he is the only coach in NCAA history to lead six universities to bowl games and the only coach to guide four different programs to the final top twenty rankings. He is a multiple winner of National Coach of the Year honors and was elected to the College Football Hall of Fame. He has also written several books. Lou is a graduate of Kent State University.

Mike Huckabee was governor of Arkansas from 1996 to 2007 and finished second in the 2008 Republican presidential primaries. He is currently hosting his own TV show and also serves as a political commentator for Fox News Channel. He also has a daily commentary, *The Huckabee Report*, on ABC Radio Networks. An ordained Southern Baptist minister, Mike is the author of six books, including the bestselling *Do the Right Thing*. He graduated magna cum laude from Ouachita Baptist University, completing his bachelor's degree in religion in two and a half years before attending Southwestern Baptist Theological Seminary.

Laurie Beth Jones is an internationally recognized bestselling author, speaker, coach, and trainer. Her business books, written from a spiritual perspective, have received global recognition. As a speaker and trainer, she has presented to presidents of countries and companies, business teams, government and the judicial system, churches and ministries, service organizations, and educators. Her book *Jesus CEO* became an international bestseller, eclipsing one million copies sold. As the owner of a successful marketing and advertising company, Laurie also consults with many individuals and organizations to help them pragmatically define and fulfill their mission. She has written several other popular books.

John Kotter has been a professor at the Harvard Business School since 1972. He has an international reputation as an authority on leadership and change. His international bestseller, *Leading Change*, became the change Bible for managers around the world. *Business Week* magazine rated him the number one "leadership guru" in America based on a survey they conducted. His reprinted articles in the *Harvard Business Review* over the past twenty years have sold more reprints—a million and a half copies—than those of any other distinguished author, and his books are in the top one percent of sales from Amazon.com. He received his bachelor's and master's degrees from MIT and earned a DBA from Harvard Business School. He joined the Harvard Business School faculty in 1972. In 1980, at the age of thirty-three, he was given tenure and a full professorship. He has written sixteen books, including *A Sense of Urgency*, *Our Iceberg Is Melting*, and *John P. Kotter on What Leaders Really Do*. He is a popular speaker and has won numerous awards for his teaching, writing, research, and innovative ideas.

Patrick Lencioni is a consultant, author, and speaker. He has written eight books, including the bestseller *The Five Dysfunctions of a Team*. Formerly at Bain & Company, Oracle, and Sybase, Patrick is currently the president of The Table Group, a management consulting firm specializing in executive team development and organizational health. As a consultant and keynote speaker, he has worked with thousands of senior executives and executive teams in organizations ranging from *Fortune* 500s and high-tech start-ups to universities and nonprofits. He speaks frequently on leadership, organizational change, teamwork, and corporate culture. *Fortune* magazine has listed him as "one of the ten new gurus you should know."

Erwin McManus is the lead pastor of Mosaic, a community of faith in Los Angeles, and heads the Mosaic Alliance, a loose association of like-minded churches. He also founded Awaken, a collection of poets, artists, filmmakers, and humanitarians whose stated goal is "maximizing the creative potential" in every human being. He has written a dozen books about culture, leadership, and postmodernism. He was named one of the fifty most influential Christians in America. He earned his BA from the University of North Carolina and his MDiv from Southwestern Baptist Theological Seminary.

Miles McPherson attended the University of New Haven, where he majored in engineering. He was the university's first player to achieve All-American honors in football and to be drafted into the NFL. He went on to play as a defensive back for the San Diego Chargers. But two years into his pro career, McPherson was battling a drug problem and living an immoral lifestyle before breaking down and eventually turning his life over to Jesus Christ. His life underwent rapid and dramatic change, resulting in his entry into ministry, working with youth. After completing his master of divinity degree at Azusa Pacific University, he founded Miles Ahead, a nonprofit organization that reaches out to America's youth. He founded Rock Church, which more than twelve thousand people attend each weekend. As one of the nation's fastest-growing churches, the Rock has sixty volunteer-led ministries that reach into the San Diego community. McPherson is the author of several books and articles, and in 2007 earned an Emmy award for a documentary on methamphetamine.

Ken Melrose served the Toro Company as president, CEO, and chairman of the board before retiring. He led the company, which was on the brink of bankruptcy when he took control, back to profitability, with sales jumping from $247 million in 1981 to nearly $2 billion annually. Under his leadership the company radically expanded its product line to serve customers in the sports, grounds management, and agricultural markets. Ken is the author of *Making the Grass Greener on Your Side: A CEO's Journey to Leading by Serving*. He earned his bachelor's degree from Princeton, a master's from the Sloan School of Management at MIT, and an MBA from the University of Chicago.

Don Soderquist joined Wal-Mart Stores, Inc., at the request of Sam Walton and served as COO and senior vice chairman. Prior to joining Wal-Mart, Soderquist served sixteen years with Ben Franklin, where he was president and CEO. He has been inducted into the Retailing Hall of Fame. In 1998, John Brown University created the Soderquist Center for Business Leadership and Ethics in his honor. The Center provides ethical leadership training for undergraduates, two master's programs (including an MBA), and business leadership seminars for people working in the corporate world. He is on the boards of various corporations and charitable organizations. Don received his BA in business administration from Wheaton College and has received several honorary doctorates.

Rich Stearns began his professional career in marketing with the Gillette Company. Subsequently, he held various roles with Parker Brothers, culminating in his appointment as president. He then served as vice president at the Franklin Mint, then joined Lenox as president of Lenox Collections. A few years later, Rich was named president and CEO of Lenox, Inc. Since leaving Lenox he has served as the president of World Vision, a Christian relief and development agency. Under Rich's direction, World Vision has experienced unprecedented growth and has become an increasingly significant player in world humanitarian aid. In addition to frequent op-ed pieces in major newspapers and magazines, he is also the author of *The Hole in Our Gospel: What Does God Expect of Us? The Answer That Changed My Life and Might Just Change the World.* Rich has a bachelor's degree from Cornell University and an MBA from the Wharton School at the University of Pennsylvania.

Lou Taylor has been the owner and CEO of Tri Star Sports and Entertainment Group for seventeen years. Tri Star is a management firm that offers business management and personal management services to professional athletes, artists, and entertainment clients. Lou is known for her "life management model," which addresses the major issues confronting celebrities, providing a solid structure to support them in all aspects of their lives. Tri Star conducts business and influences the influencers by ministering on the basis of biblical values and truths to those who are affecting pop culture. Lou is also a coauthor of the *Becoming Devotional Bible for Women.*

John Townsend is a clinical psychologist with broad experience in private practice, leadership consulting, and media. With Henry Cloud he coauthored the two-million-selling book *Boundaries.* He has written more than twenty other books, with a total of four million copies in print. John cohosts the nationally syndicated radio program *New Life Live* and conducts a leadership coaching program in southern California. He was a cofounder of Minirth-Meier ClinicWest and served as its clinical codirector for ten years, with treatment centers in thirty-five cities in the western United States. John coleads Cloud-Townsend Resources and runs a private practice with his partner, Henry Cloud. He serves on the board of various nonprofit organizations. He has a bachelor of arts degree in psychology from North Carolina State University, a master of theology degree from Dallas Theological Seminary, and a PhD in clinical psychology from Biola University.

Ralph Winter is a Hollywood film producer who has produced blockbuster movies such as the X-Men, Fantastic Four, and Star Trek series. He is also a partner in Thomas Winter Cooke, which produces television commercials and represents a number of commercial directors. A member of the Directors Guild of America and the Academy of Motion Picture Arts and Sciences, he has helped film schools at Biola University and other institutions. His first experience in production was creating training videos for Broadway Department Stores. From there he worked for Paramount Pictures Television on hit shows such as *Happy Days, Laverne & Shirley,* and *Mork and Mindy.* Ralph graduated from the University of California at Berkeley with a bachelor's degree in history.

THE MASTER LEADER LIBRARY

Many of the master leaders whose words of wisdom are contained in this book have written books that would be an invaluable addition to your leadership library. Listed below are just some of those titles for your consideration.

George Barna

The Seven Faith Tribes: Who They Are, What They Believe, and Why They Matter

The Power of Vision: Discover and Apply God's Vision for Your Life and Ministry

The Power of Team Leadership: Achieving Success through Shared Responsibility

Revolution

Warren Bennis

On Becoming a Leader

Leaders: Strategies for Taking Charge (with Burt Nanus)

Organizing Genius: The Secrets of Creative Collaboration (with Patricia Ward Biederman and Charles Handy)

Reinventing Leadership: Strategies to Empower the Organization (with Robert Townsend)

Learning to Lead (with Joan Goldsmith)

Why Leaders Can't Lead: The Unconscious Conspiracy Continues

Co-Leaders: The Power of Great Partnerships (with David Heenan)

Barry Black

From the Hood to the Hill: A Story of Overcoming

Ken Blanchard

The One Minute Entrepreneur: The Secret to Creating and Sustaining a Successful Business (with Don Hutson and Ethan Willis)

Leading at a Higher Level: Blanchard on Leadership and Creating High Performing Organizations

Lead Like Jesus: Lessons from the Greatest Leadership Role Model of All Time (with Phil Hodges)

Heart of a Leader: Insights on the Art of Influence

The One Minute Manager: The Quickest Way to Increase Your Own Prosperity (with Spencer Johnson)

Full Steam Ahead: Unleash the Power of Vision in Your Company and in Your Life (with Jesse Stoner)

Kirbyjon Caldwell

The Gospel of Good Success: A Road Map to Spiritual, Emotional, and Financial Wholeness (with Mark Seal)

Entrepreneurial Faith: Launching Bold Initiatives to Expand God's Kingdom (with Walt Kallestad and Paul Sorenson)

Ben Carson

Think Big: Unleashing Your Potential for Excellence (with Cecil Murphey)

Sam Chand

Who's Holding Your Ladder?

What's Shakin' Your Ladder? 15 Challenges All Leaders Face

Ladder Shifts: New Realities, Rapid Change, Your Destiny

Planning Your Succession: Preparing for Your Future (with Dale C. Bronner)

Henry Cloud

Boundaries: When to Say Yes, How to Say No to Take Control of Your Life (with John Townsend)

9 Things a Leader Must Do: How to Go to the Next Level—and Take Others with You

Integrity: The Courage to Meet the Demands of Reality

The One-Life Solution: Reclaim Your Personal Life While Achieving Greater Professional Success

Tony Dungy

Quiet Strength: The Principles, Practices, and Priorities of a Winning Life (with Nathan Whitaker)

Uncommon: Finding Your Path to Significance (with Nathan Whitaker)

You Can Do It

Michael Franzese

Blood Covenant: The Michael Franzese Story

I'll Make You an Offer You Can't Refuse: Insider Business Tips from a Former Mob Boss

Newt Gingrich

Real Change: From the World That Fails to the World That Works

The Art of Transformation (with Nancy Desmond)

Lessons Learned the Hard Way: A Personal Report

Winning the Future: A 21st Century Contract with America

Seth Godin

Purple Cow: Transform Your Business by Being Remarkable

Tribes: We Need You to Lead Us

Jon Gordon

The Energy Bus: 10 Rules to Fuel Your Life, Work, and Team with Positive Energy

The No Complaining Rule: Positive Ways to Deal with Negativity at Work

Training Camp: What the Best Do Better Than Everyone Else

Lou Holtz

Winning Every Day: The Game Plan for Success

Wins, Losses, and Lessons: An Autobiography

Mike Huckabee

Do the Right Thing: Inside the Movement That's Bringing Common Sense Back to America

Character Is the Issue: How People with Integrity Can Revolutionize America (with John Perry)

From Hope to Higher Ground: 12 Steps to Restoring America's Greatness

Character Makes a Difference: Where I'm From, Where I've Been, and What I Believe (with John Perry)

Laurie Beth Jones

Jesus CEO: Using Ancient Wisdom for Visionary Leadership

The Path: Creating Your Mission Statement for Work and for Life

Jesus, Life Coach: Learn from the Best (with Charles Stanley)

The Four Elements of Success: A Simple Personality Profile That Will Transform Your Life

John Kotter

A Sense of Urgency

Leading Change

Our Iceberg Is Melting: Changing and Succeeding Under Any Conditions (with Holger Rathgeber)

The Heart of Change: Real-Life Stories of How People Change Their Organizations (with Dan Cohen)

John P. Kotter on What Leaders Really Do

Power and Influence

Patrick Lencioni

The Four Obsessions of an Extraordinary Executive: A Leadership Fable

Death by Meeting: A Leadership Fable about Solving the Most Painful Problem in Business

The Five Dysfunctions of a Team: A Leadership Fable

The Five Temptations of a CEO: A Leadership Fable

The Three Signs of a Miserable Job: A Fable for Managers (and Their Employees)

Erwin McManus

Wide Awake: The Future Is Waiting within You

Soul Cravings

An Unstoppable Force: Daring to Become the Church God Had in Mind

Chasing Daylight: Seize the Power of Every Moment

Ken Melrose

Making the Grass Greener on Your Side: A CEO's Journey to Leading by Serving

Don Soderquist

The Wal-Mart Way: The Inside Story of the Success of the World's Largest Company

Live Learn Lead to Make a Difference

Rich Stearns

The Hole in Our Gospel: What Does God Expect of Us? The Answer That Changed My Life and Might Just Change the World

John Townsend

Leadership Beyond Reason: How Great Leaders Succeed by Harnessing the Power of Their Values, Feelings, and Intuition

Boundaries: When to Say Yes, How to Say No to Take Control of Your Life (with Henry Cloud)

Who's Pushing Your Button? Handling the Difficult People in Your Life

Loving People: How to Love and Be Loved

ABOUT THE AUTHORS

GEORGE BARNA has filled executive roles in politics, marketing, advertising, media development, research, and ministry. He founded the Barna Research Group in 1984 (now The Barna Group) and helped it become the leading marketing research firm focused on the intersection of faith and culture. The company has served several hundred parachurch ministries and thousands of Christian churches, as well as *Fortune* 500 companies, educational institutions, government agencies, and the military. More information about The Barna Group is accessible at www.barna.org.

To date, Barna has written more than forty books, mostly addressing leadership, cultural trends, church dynamics, and spiritual development. His books include bestsellers such as *Revolution, Pagan Christianity?* (with Frank Viola), *The Frog in the Kettle, Transforming Children into Spiritual Champions*, and *The Power of Vision*. Several of his books have received national awards. He has had more than one hundred articles published in periodicals and writes a free biweekly research report (The Barna Update) that can be accessed through his firm's Web site. His work is frequently cited as an authoritative source by the media. He has been hailed as "the most quoted person in the Christian Church today" and has been named by various media as one of the nation's most influential Christian leaders.

A popular speaker at conferences, he has taught at Pepperdine and Biola Universities and at several seminaries. Barna served as a pastor of a large multiethnic church, has been involved in several church start-ups, and presently leads a small church. He is also a frequent host and presenter on CCN, the satellite-based training network.

After graduating summa cum laude from Boston College, Barna earned two master's degrees from Rutgers University and an honorary doctorate from Dallas Baptist University. He lives with his wife and their three daughters in Southern California. His Web site is www.georgebarna.com.

BILL DALLAS is the CEO of Church Communication Network (CCN), a satellite and Internet communications company that trains leaders, clergy, and parents across North America. He is the host of *Solutions*, a weekly satellite program featuring Henry Cloud and John Townsend. Formerly a real estate developer and a Young Life leader, Bill received his bachelor's degree from Vanderbilt University. His story is told in the book he coauthored, *Lessons from San Quentin*. He lives with his wife and children in northern California. Information about CCN is available at www.ccn.tv.

INDEX

＞Available from Barna Books

Committed, born-again Christians are exiting the established church in massive numbers. Why are they leaving? Where are they going? And what does this mean for the future of the church? *Revolution* examines the state of the church today—and compares it to the biblical picture of the church as God intended it to be.

How can parents make a lasting impact on the spiritual lives of their children? To find the answer, George Barna researched the lives of thriving adult Christians and discovered the essential steps their parents took to shape their spiritual lives in childhood. *Revolutionary Parenting* shows parents how to instill in their children a vibrant commitment to Christ.

Imagine sitting down with 30 of the world's best-known and most-respected leaders as they share their hard-won insights. In *Master Leaders*, George Barna does just that—and invites us to listen in on his conversations with "the greats" (including Ken Blanchard, Tony Dungy, Newt Gingrich, Seth Godin, Lou Holtz, John Kotter, Patrick Lencioni, and many others) as they share the 16 essential leadership keys that you need to know.

Faith tribes. Everyone you know belongs to one. But each tribe stands for, and believes, very different things. In this groundbreaking book, George Barna analyzes America's seven key faith tribes—who they are, what they think, what they're passionate about, and how they're shaping our country's future.

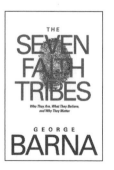

➤Available from Barna Books

Many Christians take it for granted that their church's practices are rooted in Scripture. Yet how do our practices compare to those of first-century believers? *Pagan Christianity?* leads us on a fascinating tour through history that examines and challenges every aspect of the present-day church experience.

What happens when a Christian hires an atheist to accompany him to church? Find out by following Jim Henderson's journey across the country with skeptic Matt Casper as they visit twelve of America's churches and document their experiences at and reactions to each one. Their eye-opening, entertaining dialogue opens the way for authentic, attentive friendship between Christians and nonbelievers.

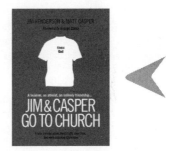

In *The Rabbit and the Elephant*, church planters Tony and Felicity Dale and acclaimed researcher George Barna use a simple analogy to bring a big message to God's church. How could we change the world if our Christian faith began multiplying at a rapid pace— through a way of life that is explosive and transformational?

A new edition of a classic work, *The House Church Book* contains everything you need to know about house churches: where they began, where they're going, how God is using them in communities around the world, and how you can start one yourself.

BARNA